M000204644

D

Finding Comfort and Guidance in a Story of a Peaceful Passing

What Readers Are Saying

"I really enjoyed reading this story. I gained a lot of insight from it. It helped me to look at my own interactions with patients and families and gave me ideas about how I could help them more."

—GINA CHAFFER, R.N., M.S.N., *Hospice nurse*

"Ever wish you had a coach to guide and encourage you when dealing with terminal illness? This touching recollection of Kris during her final months with cancer, narrated by those who cherished her, inspires through her positive coping skills and informs with practical advice not found elsewhere."

—CAROL NEWLIN, M.D., Ph.D., *psychiatrist*

"This is a book for everyone. Whether you or someone you know is currently, or was recently in the dying process this book is a useful guide to a peaceful experience. This is the warmest and most honest account of the dying process I have read. It is a guide for working with terminally ill patients as well as a story of caring and growth."

—MICHAEL JOHNSTON, L.Ac., *licensed acupuncturist*

"I found this to be an excellent way of gently communicating the importance of preparation for both dying and helping someone die. The simple examples and clear insights in this book can be helpful to people of any age, belief, education, or diagnosis."

—PEGGY WHITT, R.N., *registered nurse*

"I want to die in peace. I want to die without regret. I could understand everything you wrote. People in China would be interested in this book."

—CHUN XIAO YAN, *aesthetician*

"Thank you Dr. Underwood for taking me on an emotional journey through a dignified dying process. This is a thorough retrospect about opportunities that support people while they help a loved one die in dignity. You show how peace and light can be shared by those on their last journey with the ones left behind. You are a gifted writer, thanks for sharing."

—ORLY S. PENNY, M.Ed., *Diversity Committee, Poudre Valley Hospital System*

"This simple, eloquent, personal and professional memoir is a useful guide for those in the dying process and those helping them. For estate planning attorneys, familiarity with this book will help them counsel clients as they make choices for advance directives, living wills, durable powers and instruction for disposition of last remains."

—MARY M. DAVIS, J.D., *attorney*

"I lost my dad over 40 years ago when I was 8 years old. I wish someone had given me this information back then. This book would help anyone who has already lost someone or is about to lose someone, including the very young. I could read this book again tomorrow. It helped me understand all the deaths I've endured. It makes me more at peace about dying."

—JAN FELKER, *caregiver*

"This is great. I found it easy to read, manageable and an absolute necessity for everyone. I heard a lot of humility in the 'we learned . . .' approach which is easy to accept rather than an 'I know it all now' approach. Good job!"

—SABRÉ PAGE, *yoga teacher*

"This book is a perfect way to introduce people to the 'art of dying.' I want to give this book to everyone who comes to the funeral home. Nobody wants to talk about death. People need to allow time to plan a truly memorable service. Let's bring back some tradition and also add a new twist to the funeral process."

—ELLEN JONES, *funeral planner*

DYING

Finding Comfort and Guidance in
a Story of a Peaceful Passing

*To Dr. Coit and Dr. Wee,
With deep appreciation
for all you have done
for me ~ Judy*

JUDY K. UNDERWOOD, PH.D.

Odyssey Ink

Dying: Finding Comfort and Guidance in a Story of a Peaceful Passing
by Judy K. Underwood, Ph.D.

Odyssey Ink
515 S. Sherwood Street
Fort Collins, Colorado 80521
Phone: 970-221-0581
Fax: 970-482-8541
E-mail: DrUnderwood@passingpeacefully.com

First Printing, 2008
Copyright © 2008 by Judy K. Underwood
Cover Design © 2008 by Lightbourne, Inc., www.lightbourne.com
Front Cover Image © Stephen Coburn, 2007, used under license from Shutterstock.com

Library of Congress Control Number: 2007924284
ISBN: 978-0-9794315-1-7

To Sally and Kris
with love and gratitude

. . . She understood that the process of dying could be something more than a pathetic, morbid shuffle toward the inevitable.

— Judy Underwood

CONTENTS

FOREWORD

My father, literally, died laughing. With his children, grandchildren and great grandchildren at his bedside, his last moments arrived just as he'd planned. He wanted his loved ones close, he wanted to end his time in his physical body in joy, and he didn't take his last breath until all of us arrived.

In those final hours, my father celebrated, he laughed as heartily as he was able, he looked great – not like a man who would soon be dead. And in those final hours he provided all of us with some of the most important lessons any of us would ever learn: Death can be approached consciously, without fear and, even, with a sense of wonderment.

The way he chose to "graduate" from his life on earth to his next adventure was far different from the way most people make their transition. I am grateful that he provided me the opportunity to witness this important event.

When I received my copy of this book, I was thrilled to see author Judy Underwood taking a fresh approach to the subject of dying. The story of one woman's conscious journey toward her own death during the last year of her life is a story all of us need to read.

As a medical doctor I do not find the death of patients to be troubling. But many of my colleagues view death as some type of failure – even though 100 percent of humans die!

Judy uses the word "Dying" in her title. That took courage! Why? Because even in hospitals the medical personnel do their best to avoid using the word. They use words like: failing, passed away, ended, lost, terminated. That language shows clearly that doctors believe that a death is a failure, that somehow it can be avoided, that they can prevent it – even if the patient experiences nothing of quality from continuing to be alive.

If only they could have been at my father's bedside and learned the positive side of death. If only they would read Judy's book!

What we need to accept is that life is about beginnings. I see the death of a loved one as the chance to begin again. In all other aspects of life we view new beginnings positively. We say, "She got married!" We don't say, "She ended her life as a single woman." We say, "He had a son!" We don't say, "His life without children is over."

I see life as an eternal circle with endless beginnings. Death is not the worst outcome. While we don't know what happens to our consciousness after it is released from our physical body, what evidence do we have to doubt that the next journey is any less fantastic?

Reading Judy's story in Chapter 8 reminded me of this story from my life:

After my mother died I received a phone call from Monica, a friend of mine, who holds extraordinary mystical powers.

When she called she no longer lived near me and didn't know of my mother's death. But she received a message, and yes, I was quite surprised. When Monica called, she explained: "Your folks are together and very proud of you. They are being shown around by someone who likes cigarettes and chocolate. Do you know who that is?" I told her I didn't, and then she said, "Oh, it's Elisabeth Kübler- Ross." Elisabeth and I became close friends many years ago and she was one of my teachers. She showed me the importance of talking to anesthetized patients and departed spirits. Her teaching changed my life experience.

I accept the reality of and feel the grief that one experiences when a loved one dies. But I have learned to accept death as one of my greatest teachers. It makes me aware of my limited time here and how important it is for me to live in my heart and do what feels right for me rather than lose my life to the desires of others.

This is a poem I wrote:

THE GREAT TEACHER
Death what a great teacher you are
About life
Yet few of us elect to take your class
And learn about life
That is the essence of death's teaching
Death is not an elective
We must all take the class
The wise students audit the class in their early years
And find enlightenment
They are prepared for their commencement
When graduation day arrives

Judy can write this book because she has learned from the great teacher and is not afraid to face her mortality. She writes about the many similarities between birth and death. With the right midwives the process is much easier and free of pain.

When faced with death we need to empower ourselves and use our energy to heal our lives. This includes asking for the help we need and not denying our needs and feelings by saying, "fine" in order to please others. Dying doesn't mean you are a loser. Not experiencing life would make you a loser. Dying is inevitable and so we must choose life while we have it and live our authentic lives.

The people we love live on in our hearts and minds. I try to live the life that they would want for me and not spend it endlessly grieving. Our tears are meant to soften the dying experience but not to put out our loved one's candle. We can abandon our painful past and use it as a source of energy to move us forward in our life.

What is immortal is not success but love. Love is the bridge between the land of the living and the land of the dying.

In this book you will find, as Judy writes on the cover, "comfort and guidance in a story of a peaceful passing."

So read on and learn how to find your personal peace, help to create world peace and live in the time of your life.

Bernie Siegel, MD

ABOUT CONFIDENTIALITY

Once Kris knew she was dying, she and I talked in depth for at least an hour every Monday through Friday for eleven months—until the day before her death. We talked about her hopes, dreams, fears, regrets and frustrations. Even though I've worked as a psychotherapist for more than twenty years, this situation was different from anything I'd ever known. I was privileged to be participating in one of the most unique and intimate of all human experiences.

My work with Kris was profound; I knew we were exchanging information that would be valuable to others. When I learned she was dying, I thought of writing a book about my experiences with her.

As a therapist, I have a professional responsibility to keep all information about clients confidential. I can only share information if I have specific permission from the client for disclosure.

I didn't know how Kris would respond to my idea, so I decided to ask for her permission.

A few months before she died, I said to her, "Someday

I might want to write a book about your therapy and our experiences together. What would you think of that? I wanted to talk with you about it because I would never share information about you without your permission."

Her response was filled with delight, "Judy, that would be great. I would be so happy to help other people in that way." She signed a release-of-information form giving me permission to share anything about her that would be useful to others.

After I started writing this book, I asked her partner, Sally, how she felt about revealing personal information as part of the story. She said, "I'm comfortable with it because that's the only way for Kris to pass on her legacy. That's important to me. I like the idea of communicating with people on a deeper level. I want to let people know how meaningful the dying process can be." She also signed a release-of-information form giving me permission to share anything about her that would be useful to others.

Sally was the first person to read the finished manuscript. We agreed that she could veto any material in this book. She chose to leave everything as I wrote it, saying, "That's how it was. I want it to be authentic."

Both Kris and Sally generously shared their personal thoughts, feelings and experiences. They wanted to make the transition of dying easier for others.

I will be forever grateful to both of them for agreeing to share their stories. With their permission I am able to pass along the unique joys, sorrows and wisdom that can be found in the end-of-life experience.

THE BEGINNING

In the spring of 2003, I sat at my desk entering process notes on the computer for my last client of the day. At the same time, I hit the speakerphone button and listened to my voicemail. Multi-tasking had become a way of life. My habits had changed considerably since my early years as a psychotherapist when I hired an answering service to take calls and used a typewriter to make notes.

I found my work satisfying and enjoyed my busy practice. I was the ultimate self-employed therapist taking on various roles and responsibilities during the course of the day. In addition to working with clients, I did all my own secretarial and administrative tasks. I was proud of my work and the level of service I provided to my clients. They knew they could count on me.

As I listened to messages that day, I wrote down notes and phone numbers so I could return calls as soon as possible. Everything seemed routine until I heard Sally's voice.

Many years ago when her partner, Kris, asked me to work with Sally, I declined. At that time Kris had been my client for nine years. She had worked through numerous complex issues stemming from her tumultuous childhood. I didn't want to risk creating a relationship with Sally that might interfere with Kris's work. I also didn't want to risk the possibility of Sally and Kris competing for my attention.

Sally had made little progress during years of therapy with numerous therapists. Kris pointed out to me that these were unusual circumstances. Both Kris and Sally talked with me convincingly about all the reasons I should work with Sally. Finally, I agreed to accept her as a client on a trial basis.

That was eleven years ago and none of us ever regretted that decision. We were all grateful for the way events unfolded.

The tone of Sally's voice grabbed my attention. I knew something was seriously wrong. She said in a scared, child-like voice, "Kris is in emergency surgery, and I'm at the hospital waiting." In all the years I'd known them, neither had ever had a medical emergency. Both appeared to be in excellent physical health, so this was a complete surprise.

Twenty years earlier, Sally had completed a program to become a Licensed Practical Nurse (LPN). Although she was never employed as a nurse, her training helped her feel more comfortable in the hospital and around doctors.

I hung up the phone and immediately picked up the receiver again to call the hospital. Even without the details, I knew this surgery would be life-altering for both Kris and Sally. What I didn't know was how much it would change my life. In the next few weeks we learned that Kris's illness was terminal.

For the following eleven months I immersed myself in her dying process. Because I had neither training nor experience in end-of-life issues, I threw myself into the study of death and dying with books, tapes and consultations with others. I cared deeply about Kris and knew she would not trust anyone else to help with this process. She trusted me as much as she trusted anyone and I was committed to helping her in any way I could. I realized that to help her I needed to learn a lot in a hurry.

During those months I was fascinated by the similarities between death and birth. I wished for a word comparable to "pregnancy" to describe the dying time. Both of these lifecycle events are significant transitions. For the birthing process, prospective parents can choose help from midwives, doctors, nurses or doulas. These people help us create the birth experience we want.

In an ideal world all people would have help finding a way to die that is right for them. Help would come from a friend, relative, neighbor, colleague, healthcare provider, spiritual leader or personal coach. I knew there was not one right way to die. What I didn't know yet was what choices were available. Going through the journey toward death with Kris helped reinforce my belief that we all deserve a dying process that meets our own special needs.

Kris had just celebrated her 56th birthday at the time of her diagnosis. Because cancer had spread from her colon to her liver, she decided against chemotherapy. She wanted to make the most of her remaining time. Kris had known people who had subjected themselves to the torturous rigor of chemotherapy. Even if it lengthened her life by a few days, weeks, months or years she didn't want that experience. She saw the miserable side effects chemotherapy produced.

Instead, she chose to focus the time she had left on completing her life without regret—and with as much comfort as possible.

I remember when Kris said to me, "Judy, I want to have a good death and I want you to help make it happen."

Overwhelmed with warm feelings toward her I had no hesitation when I said, "Yes, we'll do that together."

This book is Kris's legacy—the story of the last eleven months of her life. More importantly, it's what I'm passing on to you in the hope that when you find yourself facing the end of life—either your own or a loved one's—you can handle the situation with equanimity. You will be able to go through the dying time with no regrets rather than looking back wishing you had done it differently.

Notice I said "when" not "if." One of my epiphanies is that it does no good to be in denial about death. The vast majority of us will know weeks or months in advance that we are near the end of life. So why not be prepared?

My fervent wish is that this book will serve as a compassionate guide to help you navigate the transition with dignity. Whether you are helping someone through the process—or facing the end of your own life—this book can help you find the insights, strength and clarity to create the meaningful experience that you deserve.

EVERYONE
DIES

It may seem odd that at the end of this first chapter I will ask you to answer some questions. Most books that explore personal issues save the questions for the end.

The reason I've chosen to take this different approach is because I know it will be useful for you to examine your most basic feelings about death before you start reading this book.

Most of us choose to keep our fear of and questions about death well hidden in our psychic closets. That choice, of course, is understandable. Thinking about death is not prized as a pleasurable experience.

When we consider death we are confronted with many questions, most of which cannot be answered. Consequently, avoiding the questions is much easier than confronting them.

We all know that at some time in our lives we must consider death and attempt to reach some type of personal understanding. Not talking about death won't make it go away. Death is a certainty. The only uncertainties regarding your death and my death are how and when we will die.

Death is an inevitable passage. By facing it, we remove its power to loom over our lives. Many people face death alone and in absolute confusion and terror. This happens at a time in life when emotions are often overwhelming. Dying is a time when we have to make numerous life and death decisions—literally and figuratively. There is no one right decision, and decisions made at this time can be extremely difficult.

I am no different from most people. I waited to confront the questions about death until the realities of end-of-life issues were thrown into my face without warning.

This book provides the very personal story of how I helped Kris prepare to die well—in her words, "to die a good death." The experience launched me on an incredible journey for which I was not prepared. The journey was unbelievably difficult and shockingly satisfying.

Most people, at some time, talk about living well. All of us have our own definitions of what that means. In contrast, the idea of dying well presents concepts that few people have ever considered.

Kris made an astounding choice to face her death in a very conscious manner. While she didn't know exactly what that meant, she understood that the process of dying could be something more than a pathetic, morbid shuffle toward the inevitable.

This is not to say that Kris enjoyed the thought of dying, or the physical and emotional pain that accompanied the process. But by acknowledging that her life was ending and by making a commitment to a process of dying, Kris avoided the pointless struggle of fighting death. Instead, she lived fully to the end.

Many people have written about what it means to die well. Some say that dying well means going through the process without physical pain and without suffering. Some say that it means dying with dignity and completing life without regret. Some say it means dying with the help of and in the presence of loved ones.

As each of us has defined what it means to live well, each of us can develop a definition of what it means to die well. Reading about death and considering death doesn't mean that we've given up on life. Dying doesn't mean that we've failed. Planning for our own death won't hasten the process. Everyone dies. Engaging in a conscious process facilitates a peaceful passing. Contrary to what most people believe, the dying process does not need to be a time of pain, suffering and loneliness. There is humor and hope and love in this process.

In this story, I give many details about Kris's life and about how she and Sally handled the process and accompanying issues. I offer details because in all lives and deaths there are commonalities. By observing the actions of others we learn something about ourselves. By reading about someone else's experience of dying well, it is my hope that you'll determine the experience that you want or help loved ones achieve the experiences they want.

Below you will find eight questions. My purpose in asking you to answer them is to provide a stepping-off point for your own incredible journey.

Please, take the time to answer these questions. They may appear, at first, to be difficult. But as you think about them and respond, you will begin to understand that it is possible to die well.

These questions are not meant to be morbid. There are no right or wrong answers. My intention is to bring death out of the closet and to help you start conversations about it. By answering these questions and discussing them with loved ones, you can deepen your relationships—with them and with yourself.

I suggest you write the answers. You may copy pages 4–6, and please take your time.

1. What is your definition of dying well?

_____

_____

_____

_____

_____

2. How do you want to be remembered after you die?

_____

_____

_____

_____

_____

3. What are three words you would use to describe death?

_____

_____

_____

4. What experiences have you had with death, and how do they influence you now?

_____

_____

_____

_____

_____

_____

_____

5. What is your belief about what happens after death?

_____

_____

_____

_____

_____

6. *If you had a terminal illness, how would you want to handle it?*

_____

_____

_____

_____

_____

_____

7. *Are you willing to create a plan for dealing with your own death, put it in writing and discuss it with at least one other person?*

_____

_____

_____

_____

_____

_____

8. *If you answered yes to question 7, when will you do it?*

_____

_____

_____

_____

_____

2

THE DIAGNOSIS
& TREATMENT
DECISIONS

I stared at the date on my phone message log. I had written 5/21 in the upper right-hand corner while my voicemail system was connecting to messages. My adrenaline rushed as I heard Sally's voice. She was calling me from the hospital, and she sounded anxious and scared. I returned the call immediately and waited nervously as I was transferred many times. Finally, I was connected to the appropriate nurses' station, where I was able to talk directly with Sally.

She brought me up to date, telling me what happened in the past three days. "Kris had acute abdominal pain on Monday, and we went to her doctor. She was dehydrated and we spent a few hours there while she was given an IV of saline solution. That helped her feel somewhat better. She didn't sleep much that night, and the next morning her abdominal pain was worse. We went back to her doctor and were sent to the hospital for a CT scan. After the CT scan, the doctor met us at the hospital, where we had a consultation with a surgeon. The four of us went into a tiny room, where the surgeon lifted Kris's shirt and felt her abdomen.

"He said, 'The CT scan shows a bowel obstruction. You'll need to go into surgery.'

"You know how Kris is about doctors and hospitals. She said, 'OK, I'll go home and think about it.'

"Kris's doctor and the surgeon looked at her and together they said, 'No, Now!' They were concerned her colon could burst.

"It was only because she was in severe pain that she agreed to surgery. She was taken to pre-op, where she was in bed in a big room with other patients. The beds were separated only by curtains. I waited with her for over an hour before they took her into surgery. They escorted me to a waiting room."

On the phone I was in my therapist mode. My focus was totally on Sally, listening to what she said and hearing what she didn't say, too. I knew she was feeling tired and scared. All my attention was on her and helping her cope with this crisis. I wasn't aware of my own feelings. At least, not yet. I made a plan with Sally to keep in touch by phone and let her know I would come to the hospital as soon as Kris wanted to see me.

Later, I thought about how someone's whole world can change in an instant. Joan Didion, best-selling author, wrote about her experience in the weeks and months following her husband's sudden death from a massive coronary. This is what she wrote in her book *The Year of Magical Thinking*:

Life changes fast.

Life changes in the instant.

You sit down to dinner and life as you know it ends.

▲ ▲ ▲

After about an hour and a half, the surgeon told Sally the operation had gone well. He knew Kris was sick with cancer even without a pathology report—and he explained that to Sally. He drew a diagram showing where he had made the incision. Initially, Sally thought that the cancer was curable. He told her where she could find Kris's hospital room. Sally waited for Kris in the empty room.

"It seemed like I waited there forever," Sally told me.

When they finally brought Kris to her room, she was groggy. Sally spent the night at the hospital. Eventually a cot was brought in for her, and they were there for the next six days. During that time an oncologist made two visits. She introduced herself and gave them written information. She explained that Kris had Stage III colon cancer, talked about how common it was and described treatment options.

The hospital staff treated Sally respectfully and did not raise any questions about her and Kris being a couple. It seemed Fort Collins, a Colorado agricultural town once known for its conservative politics, had caught up with the times. Everyone at the hospital accepted the women's partnership.

Initially, the doctors recommended chemotherapy. But as more tests were done, they learned that the cancer had spread to her liver. The diagnosis changed—Stage IV colon cancer. That meant the cancer had advanced to the point where the value of chemotherapy was questionable.

With that knowledge Kris displayed her characteristic ability to make decisions quickly and without anyone else's consultation. She decided immediately to spend as much time as she could feeling good in the time she had left rather than trying to extend her life. Chemotherapy, she said, would not be an option.

Kris accepted that she was dying.

She said emphatically, "I am not having chemotherapy. I'm not going down that road."

Some people believe that we are given a number of possible exit points to leave our lives on earth. They think some of those times are opportunities when we can choose life or death. Kris recognized this as an exit point, and she knew it was time for her to leave.

When Kris came to me and said, "Judy, I want to die a good death," I was taken aback. I didn't know what that meant. In that one sentence she presented a concept that would forever change my life. Throughout the next eleven months, as I thought about "a good death," my perspective on life and death changed.

I asked Kris what dying a good death meant to her. She explained that she wanted to feel a sense of completion about her life and resolve unfinished business with people from her past and with those she knew in the present. She wanted to live this last phase of her life from a place of love. She wanted to prepare emotionally and spiritually for the moment of death and the time right afterwards when she believed her soul would be traveling to "the other side."

Acceptance of dying is a critical part of planning to die well. If she had been in denial about dying or if she'd been fighting death, all her energy would have been aimed at staying alive instead of living in the love that she felt in the present moment. Given her conviction that she wanted to approach death consciously, we were able to talk about what it meant to her to die well and what needed to be done to make it happen.

I was surprised when a few months after her diagnosis Kris said, "Judy, this is the best time of my life." It never occurred to me that could be so.

During this last year of her life, loved ones gave her plenty of attention, people catered to her and medical providers prescribed medicine to manage her pain. We supported her and accepted whatever she wanted to do— including continuing to smoke. Sally and I referred to her as "Queen Kris."

Kris had been a smoker for almost forty years. We knew smoking caused lung cancer and throat cancer—those consequences of tobacco use were well publicized. As I did research, I learned from the American Cancer Society that smoking also causes other kinds of cancers. This information made sense to all of us, since carcinogens go through the entire body, including the colon.

Given Kris's diagnosis, we all knew that quitting smoking at this time would yield little, if any, benefit.

While she could still drive, walk and get around, Kris went to the oncologist's office every six weeks. These visits allowed the doctor to monitor Kris's condition. She asked me to come with her and Sally to help process any feelings about what happened during each visit. She wanted me to make sure that she wasn't missing anything important and that the oncologist wasn't omitting any information. The doctor was supportive, checked her physically, answered questions and prescribed medicine. She was very welcoming each time Kris, Sally and I came to her office. She joked with Kris and always treated her respectfully.

As Kris's abdomen got bigger and bigger, the doctor reassured us that this was the normal course of the illness. She told Sally, "You get to go shopping again. Kris needs new clothes."

Six weeks after her emergency surgery and eight months before she died, Kris started asking people to visit her instead of her going to see them. Both her chiropractor and her hair dresser made home visits. She stopped going to the doctor's office. Instead, the Hospice nurse came to their home once a week. The nurse communicated with the doctor and made all the arrangements about medicine. In the last weeks of Kris's life, the Hospice nurse came more often.

When Kris asked me if I would make home visits, she was being mindful of her priorities with her limited energy. This was a situation where she could still exercise control of her life.

Kris saved her energy for going out to restaurants with Sally. For many years they had structured their life together around their daily restaurant meals. Even though Sally would have preferred to eat at home more often, they both valued the deep conversations and meaningful connection they had when they ate out. They went to a few restaurants consistently and enjoyed the special attention they got as regular patrons. Because it was so important to Kris, the couple made going out to eat a top priority until she died.

While the couple's lives changed in an instant, Kris's treatment decision set a path that guided the remainder of their days together. That path allowed them to live fully and remain engaged in the activities they enjoyed—it allowed them to continue the normal routines of their lives.

3

TAKING PICTURES

L ate one afternoon about a month after Kris had been diagnosed, I sat at the hair salon with the vinyl cape around my shoulders. My feet were propped up on the metal foot rest of the hydraulic chair in front of the big mirror. That day I barely noticed all the familiar smells of the salon or the sound of country-western music in the background. Dianne had been my hairdresser for more than twenty years, and I considered her a dear friend.

During Kris's illness, Dianne was one of the people I turned to for guidance because her mother had died of cancer, and she'd listened to many of her clients talk about their loved ones dying.

When she asked me how I was feeling, all my emotions spilled out. "I really want to help her die in a good way. I hope I can do it."

Then she suggested something that had not occurred to me.

She said, "Judy, you have to get pictures of her while she's still looking good. She won't want to have pictures taken when she's looking sick. And her partner won't want to look at those. That's not what she'll want to remember."

Her idea was brilliant. I realized how important that would be for Sally. I also thought it could be fun and didn't even consider that it might be painful. If we didn't take the pictures, I knew it would be something that we'd regret later.

More than a year after Kris died, I learned even more about the importance of those photographs.

Once Kris recovered from surgery, I suggested a photo session to her and Sally. They hesitated at first; but they understood the significance of the idea. A couple of days after I made the suggestion, we set a date for me to come to their home.

We took pictures in meaningful places. For example, I took a picture of Kris and Sally in front of the entryway to their home. Sally took a picture of Kris and me sitting on a favorite stone bench.

At first the session was strained. But after a few minutes, we all loosened up and simply enjoyed the moment. We put aside worries about Kris's illness and focused on the project together. No one talked about the past or the future.

More than a year after Kris died, Sally told me of the strong emotions she experienced that day. Her explanation showed me the importance of setting up moments that will help families and partners remember meaningful times with their loved ones.

With tears in her eyes, Sally said, "We both knew why we were taking these pictures, and that they would be the last ones. It was so different from how it usually was. With vacation pictures we were happy, and we knew there would be more vacations and more pictures."

She continued, "Kris knew these pictures were really important. They had more significance. She was very careful to wear the right clothes. She made sure the sun was just right. She paid attention to the background. She was fully engaged. Usually when we took pictures, she was more casual.

"I loved it that she was that way. It was hard. We were so aware of the reason for these pictures. We took a whole bunch. Taking these pictures made it more real that she was going to die. I think it was a lot harder for me than for Kris. It was another expression of her acceptance of her upcoming death."

I asked, "She was more accepting than you?"

"Oh, yeah. I just marveled at that because she was so young. Less than a month ago she had turned fifty-six, and the next thing I knew—she was dying. I would have been fighting it the whole way. It was hard for me to grasp how she could accept her own death. And it was comforting to me that she was so accepting. It gave me peace of mind to know she was peaceful about dying. It would have been traumatic for both of us if she'd been fighting a losing battle."

I asked Sally to tell me more about her experience taking the pictures.

"With those pictures I started thinking, this is proof she was really here. Taking those pictures was sad. At the same time it was a celebration of her life and a marker that she was really here.

"What I wanted with those pictures was a last memory of how she looked before she started looking sick. Having those pictures was reassuring and comforting. They helped me remember how she looked before she got sick.

"We didn't say any words about why we were taking the pictures. We didn't need to, and we didn't want to."

I wanted to hear more. "Sally, tell me about your experience after you printed the pictures."

She said, "We studied them and said what we liked about them. Then Kris put them in the photo album. It was a relief to have the pictures and have the project done. It was hard to do that and nice to have it over. It was so important to have the pictures. They were a recognition of her."

Sally thought about what the pictures meant to Kris. "I think the pictures were important to her, too. I wish we had talked about that. I wish I had asked her. Maybe they were important to her in the same way. Maybe she liked it that they were a recognition of her. She was here.

"These pictures were so important because I knew I would never see her again. They were the only way I could ever see her again. I knew there would be a huge void. I was losing a big part of my life."

Sally sounded so helpless as she recalled the feelings she'd had before Kris died. I said to her, "You had no voice, no say in the matter, and there was nothing you could do about it."

"Yes," she said, "and I could only stand by and watch it all happen."

"It must have been a very powerless feeling," I said.

She nodded her head, yes.

Once she acknowledged her feelings of powerlessness, she allowed herself to experience her anger. She even raised her voice, which she seldom does.

"I was supposed to accept Kris's death and go along with something I didn't want. I was supposed to be cheery about taking pictures, and I was pissed as hell. I didn't want to do anything that would acknowledge Kris's death. I didn't want to go along with her acceptance. And if I did agree to her point of view, I wanted to go along kicking and screaming the whole way."

I could tell she was relieved to express her anger.

Calmly, she added, "Yet, I never showed my objection in any way. I just went along."

Sally thought for a moment and then said, "I would guess it was a lot easier for Kris to take those pictures than for me. She was accepting of the death and I wasn't. She thought the pictures were a great idea. I knew I was sad at the time. Only now I'm realizing I was angry, too."

"Oh, Sally," I said, "I wish back then I had said to you, 'How is it for you to be taking these pictures?'"

She looked stricken, "Yowee! I would have fallen apart."

"How does it feel to talk about it now?" I asked her.

"It's good. I'm liking it. I didn't realize I had all these feelings. Behind my anger, I was so hurt because she was going to leave me," she responded.

I asked Sally about the photo album.

"I have the photo album in my library. I like having it there. My library is a place of peace and serenity, a place for introspection and learning, a place for being. Kris's photo albums fit in with that environment. They are a part of introspection and part of being. They represent twenty-four years of my life, and they represent who Kris was. She was such an important part of my life."

She continued, "It was Kris who taught me to be introspective and how to *be* instead of *do*. I was always doing things. She often talked to me about *being* instead of *doing*. Even though I couldn't do that while she was here, she taught me all about it. She taught me about learning in all ways. She demonstrated her values of personal growth and learning by talking and by how she lived her life. I learned so much from her."

After a slight pause, Sally mentioned the importance of including me in the pictures.

"It was a day to treasure when the three of us were together."

Sally's comments made me reflect on the relationship the three of us had with each other. I was aware of the acceptance, respect, care and support present in every direction among the three of us.

Sally admitted to some confusion when she thought about the photo session. While she appeared to enjoy that morning, she also felt sadness and anger. She wondered if taking the pictures was difficult for Kris.

"We never talked about our feelings that day. There was so much we talked about and now I'm realizing there was also so much we didn't talk about. I'm sorry for the missed opportunities. We were so focused on doing. There was so much to do to take care of Kris and deal with all that needed to be done. Sometimes you run out of gas. There's only so much talking and doing you can do."

I told her, "Really it doesn't matter that we didn't talk about everything. You can trust the process."

As Sally and I talked, she thought of many more questions. But even as she wondered about something she knew she'd never be able to answer, she understood the importance of those pictures and the significance of that time we spent together taking photographs.

4

TELLING OTHERS

At first, Kris didn't want anyone besides Sally and me to know she had cancer. They talked with me from the beginning and kept me updated as they learned new information about Kris's condition. I helped them decide how they wanted to proceed with each new step.

While Kris was in the hospital, her sister called a few times and left messages on their home phone. Toward the end of the week, her sister's messages were pointed, "Hey, you guys I know something's up. Call me and let me know what's going on."

Sally told Kris about the messages and Kris replied, "I'll call her back when I'm ready." Neither one of them called her back for almost a week.

Kris and Sally had always been a private couple; they saw no immediate reason to change their behavior.

Sally said, "We knew we weren't ready to tell anyone but you. We were trying to get a handle on it ourselves. In the hospital we were focused on getting Kris to pass gas. We weren't ready to grapple with the world. The deal was that when she could pass gas, she could go home. It took all our energy to keep Kris comfortable—going to the bathroom, giving her pain medicine, taking her outside for cigarettes, checking her vital signs, working with the respiratory therapist. All our focus was on her recovery from surgery, and she was high maintenance. We didn't want to deal with anyone else. We didn't know what it all meant."

Kris wanted to be the one to tell her sister. It was hard for Sally not to respond to the voicemail messages. She knew she wouldn't be able to call back and pretend everything was OK when it wasn't. So the messages went unanswered until after Kris came home from the hospital.

Within a week of coming home—she'd been in the hospital for six days—Kris announced, "I'm going to call my sister now."

On the phone with her sister she moved right to the point, "I had to have emergency surgery because of a bowel obstruction, and it turned out to be colon cancer. We're in the process of considering different treatment options."

Her sister, who is a nurse, asked a lot of medical questions. Kris and Sally knew she'd ask those questions, and they shared everything they'd been told.

After Kris died, her sister told us, "As soon as I heard the diagnosis of colon cancer, I knew it was the end." She never let on that she knew. She wanted Kris to go through her own process.

Kris wanted other family members to know, but she didn't want to be the one to tell them. Emotionally it was hard for her to acknowledge her own vulnerability, and she didn't have the energy to deal with other people's reactions. The first time we met with the Hospice counselor, he brought up the topic of telling others. He said, "Once you start telling others, you'll find that other people will share their stories and it can help you feel not so alone, and you'll get helpful information."

We found that was true. I ran into a colleague at the gym who recommended *Life on the Other Side,* a book by Sylvia Browne. Because I was educating myself about death and dying as fast as I could, I bought the book that day.

Browne is a psychic and her books are written from that perspective. They presented a point of view that was new to me, and I wasn't sure how Kris and Sally would respond to those ideas. After finishing that book, I told Kris about it and asked her if she was interested in looking at it. She borrowed it and after reading *Life on the Other Side,* she subsequently read Browne's *Blessings From the Other Side.* Kris and Sally found these books reassuring and comforting during Kris's illness.

I knew it was important for Kris and Sally to tell people about Kris's situation for other reasons, too. Talking about her terminal cancer diagnosis made it more real. That helped both women shed their denial and face the truth. While Kris decided quickly not to attempt to extend her life, nearly six months passed before they totally accepted that Kris was dying. Acceptance was a key ingredient in helping Kris create the "good death" that she wanted. As they both grew to acceptance, they found it helpful to talk about the situation with others.

If Kris had kept her diagnosis secret, she would have added stress to an already stressful situation. Some people who are dying are reluctant to tell others in an effort to protect themselves or their listeners from uncomfortable feelings. In truth, lying and hiding information creates more uncomfortable feelings.

Here's an extreme example—a friend told me about a woman who died of breast cancer. She refused to tell her closest family members about her illness because of her tremendous shame in having cancer. Her religion taught her that if she prayed hard enough she would be healed from any disease. To her, the progression of her illness meant she was a failure, and she didn't want anyone to think of her that way. Because of her insistence on secrecy, she died without people around her who would have given her love and support. She died believing she was a failure. After her death, when her friends and family learned what had happened, they felt sad and angry. They felt cheated out of the opportunity to give her their love and caring.

Telling others deepens relationships. Kris wanted to be truthful. People consistently responded to her with love, caring, support and encouragement. These conversations enriched her life significantly, thus changing her at the end of her life. As she opened up to people and shared the truth of her profound experience, she personified love. Her energy attracted unconditional love from others. During the last eleven months of her life, many people commented on the changes they noticed in Kris. They saw her calm, peaceful, loving demeanor.

Kris, Sally and I developed a pattern of letting other people know about her illness. First, Kris decided which people she wanted to know. Next, Kris or Sally would tell the people closest to them and ask them to tell others. Lastly, when they couldn't bring themselves to share the information with someone, I talked with that person. Because I was one step removed from Kris and Sally, some people found it easier to hear the news from me than from them. This worked well. These people could react without having to worry about how their responses would affect Kris and Sally.

When friends had questions they didn't feel comfortable asking Kris or Sally, they could ask me. Sometimes people didn't know how to respond to the news. Giving them the opportunity to talk with me helped them feel more comfortable. Then they could respond the way they wanted when they talked with Kris and Sally.

Kris's list of people to tell about her illness included her family of origin, Sally's family of origin, current friends, friends she hadn't seen for a long time and some other people she saw regularly.

Kris and Sally knew that Kris's immediate family would be the first they would tell. Kris's family included two sisters and her mother—all living far away. Kris had already told the sister to whom she felt closest. At Kris's request, her sister told their other sister and their mother. Kris knew the news would spread to her extended family of nieces and nephews. When there were children involved, the parents of the children explained the situation.

Both of Kris's sisters thought it best not to tell their elderly mother. She had been living in a nursing home for many years, and they worried she wouldn't be able to handle the news. Kris didn't agree with this decision and at the same time didn't have the energy to fight. She had strong feelings about telling the truth no matter how difficult.

I went with Kris and Sally to numerous doctor appointments. During one visit, I brought up the issue of telling her mother. One of her doctors quoted research which showed people needed about three months to accept the news that someone is dying. They need that time to come to terms with the impending loss.

I urged Kris to tell her mother. Again, Kris told her sister that she wanted her mother to know the truth.

After much discussion, Kris's sisters made arrangements to travel to the nursing home and tell their mother. They used the straightforward approach, telling her of the emergency surgery and the diagnosis of colon cancer. They told her it had spread to Kris's liver and they didn't know how much longer she would live. They assured her that Kris was getting the best possible care and was surrounded by love and support.

Because they knew her mother would have a difficult time with the news, they discussed the situation with her doctor and arranged to have a sedative available. This proved to be wise preparation. Kris's mother needed sedatives for many days. Even though breaking the news was difficult, it gave her time to accept her daughter's medical condition. She wrote numerous letters to Kris saying good-bye.

After Kris's family was told, Sally wanted her family to know. Sally called her parents and told them. She also called her oldest sister, who had been like a second mother to her, and asked her to let others in the family know. Sally's extended family included three other siblings, many young adults in the next generation and their children.

In her phone calls, she explained the situation in the same straightforward manner we'd used with everyone else.

Sally said, "Telling others was hard, and it was good at the same time. It was hard because of all the intense feelings that came up each time we told someone. It was hard dealing with our own feelings and also dealing with the feelings and reactions of the other person."

Kris was not very social. The couple had many friends and acquaintances, but mostly they kept to themselves. Kris realized, however, how important it was to reach out to old friends and family because she worried about how Sally would cope after she died. Kris told her, "I want to bring people back into our life so you'll have them in your life after I'm gone. I'm doing this for you—not for me."

Sally liked that. She wanted to have these people back in her life, and at the time she felt incapable of doing that for herself.

Kris started by calling old friends they hadn't seen for many years and arranged to meet for lunch. Even though the friendships had not been nurtured, the old acquaintances cautiously accepted the invitation. All of them were nervous when they met at the restaurant.

In her straightforward way Kris cleared the air quickly, "I had to go in for emergency surgery, and I have terminal colon cancer."

At first the friends were speechless. After comprehending the news they replied, "I'm so glad you told us. Is there anything we can do?"

Kris said, "We would like your friendship."

They said, "Of course, we're here for you." Sally was glad Kris had arranged that lunch. She appreciated the connection, the friendship and the support offered.

At the end of that meeting, Kris asked their friends to tell other friends. The news spread through the community. Soon, other people called and said, "I just heard the news. What can I do?"

Kris and Sally felt love and support from many old friends. Although telling people was hard, it was worth the effort. Kris and Sally enjoyed feeling connected with friends again.

Some people were told about Kris's illness in the normal course of life's daily events. For example, when Sally went to the dentist, she cancelled Kris's appointment and told the dentist and receptionist of Kris's terminal illness. Sally told their chiropractor, and he offered to make a home visit. That was helpful in keeping Kris comfortable during a particular stage of her illness. When their plumber came to install a hand-held shower, Sally met him at the door and explained the situation to him before he came into the house.

Kris and Sally had become friendly with one of the checkers at the grocery store. One day when it wasn't very busy, Kris told her, "I recently had emergency surgery. They found terminal colon cancer." The checker's eyes filled with tears. She came around the check-out stand and embraced Kris. It was as if time stood still.

By being truthful, Kris brought an act of love into her life. The hug from the friend in the grocery store was one of hundreds Kris received in the last months of her life.

A discussion with one friend took a surprising turn. Kris worked with a contractor for years doing various home remodeling projects. She wanted him to know about her illness and planned to tell him for many weeks. But she could never bring herself to tell him. He was working at my house at the time, and I knew it would be easy for me to talk to him.

"Kris, do you want me to tell him for you?" I asked.

She seemed relieved as she nodded her head. I told him in the same direct way Kris told everyone. The contractor and I talked for a long time and gave each other caring and support. Later, Kris invited him over for tea. During the visit he started to talk to Kris and Sally about his religion—a topic they never talked about when they worked on projects together. The man's comments surprised and upset Kris and Sally; neither of them had been prepared for that. They told me about the incident and how uncomfortable they had been. At their request, I intervened.

A few days later when I saw him, I explained that while some people found comfort in talking about religion, Kris and Sally found it disturbing. I acknowledged his positive intentions. I asked him if he was willing not to talk about religion with them again. He agreed.

This incident helped us all be more prepared for someone reacting in a way that was especially upsetting. I learned to be ready to say, "Excuse me, I need to interrupt you. I understand that could be comforting to some people and that your intentions are good. Talking about religion is disturbing to Kris and Sally. Please stop. Thanks for being respectful about that."

After Kris died, when I talked with Sally about telling other people about Kris's terminal illness she said, "When we told people, they were shocked, but they didn't fall off their chairs or anything. It doesn't have to be hard to talk about this. It's not something to be scared of."

5

TALKING ABOUT
DEATH

By November, six months after Kris's diagnosis, we had already moved our daily sessions to her home. She had given away her exercise equipment and turned her workout room into a sitting room with two comfortable recliners. As she and I each sat in one of the chairs, I appreciated the spacious view of the large field next to their home with the mountains in the distance.

Whatever people believe about death and dying influences their experience at the end of life. For that reason, it's important for people who are dying to express those beliefs. Their thoughts can contribute to a calm, peaceful experience, or they can fuel fear or terror. Talking about their beliefs allows people to voice their hopes, dreams and fears about their final transition. Conversations provide an opportunity to get support and reassurance that they don't have to go through this process alone. Yet, if they prefer to be alone at the moment of death, they can arrange that, too.

Facing fears directly often makes them less scary. I knew if Kris had specific fears, we would figure out a plan to deal with them. I had no way of knowing what Kris believed without asking her directly.

"Can we talk about death?" I asked Kris.

"I suppose it's a good idea," she said.

Even though she knew she would die soon, she wouldn't have brought up this topic on her own.

"Tell me your beliefs about death. What are your thoughts about what happens at the moment of death and right afterwards?"

At first, Kris didn't respond. Perhaps my question was too general or maybe she had too many thoughts and didn't know what to say first. I waited patiently, comfortable being together in the silence.

After a few moments she told me that right after she died, she expected to be welcomed by people and animals she had known who had already died. She envisioned them greeting her as she arrived on "the other side." Her thoughts of reuniting with her deceased pets gave her great comfort.

There were times when she was agitated and fearful. I asked, "Are you more uncomfortable with the thought of dying or what will happen afterwards?"

Her response was immediate, "I'm not afraid of dying. I don't think there will be much pain. I'm afraid of getting lost and going to the wrong place. I don't want to be in a situation where I'm surrounded by bad people. I know that after I die I'm supposed to go to a specific place where it's beautiful and peaceful. I'm just scared I might have trouble getting there."

"Are you thinking of heaven and hell?" I asked.

"Well, I don't really believe in hell, but I suppose maybe it's something like that," she said.

While most people avoid talking about their fears, addressing them directly is an important way to overcome them. I encouraged Kris to talk about her fears by saying, "Tell me more about what's going on in your mind about hell."

She talked about terrifying images of the fires of hell she'd developed during childhood. They were associated with statements about evil, sin and damnation that she'd heard at church. She vaguely remembered hearing things about "Satan," "Lucifer" and "The Devil" but hadn't thought about them for many years. Even though she had dismissed those concepts years ago, they were haunting her as her own death approached. She told me those memories were fuzzy, and she didn't want to remember them. She had worked hard to repress those memories and I honored her wish to leave them alone.

My focus was to help her take charge of her thoughts and beliefs. I wanted her to know that she could believe whatever she wanted and whatever would be best for her.

I said to her, "Of course, there's no way to know for sure exactly what happens after death. We have many stories from people who were declared dead and then came back to life. There are books about that. There are psychics who tell us of their communications with people who have died.

"Kris, what do you *want* to believe about what happens after death? What beliefs would be most helpful and comforting to you now?"

I asked her to describe in detail what she wanted to happen after her death. I encouraged her to focus on how she wanted it to be instead of how she was scared it might be or how someone else told her it would be.

For a few minutes she stayed silent and focused on what she wanted to happen at the moment of her death. Then she said, "I want to die peacefully in my sleep. I want to be greeted by all the loving animals I've had over the years, and I want someone to help my spirit make the transition from this place to the next. I want someone to guide me to the beautiful place where I'm supposed to go next. There I will see many beings of goodness, and I will be one of them. I will be young and healthy again."

When she talked about the concepts of heaven and hell, those frightened her and served no useful purpose. In contrast, when she talked about how angels would guide her to a beautiful place where she was healthy and vibrant, she felt peaceful.

Because Kris, Sally and I all read Sylvia Browne's books about life "on the other side," we had a shared spiritual view of death. Browne describes a healing place where one's spirit goes directly after the death of the body. There the spirit will complete the healing it couldn't accomplish on earth. Her books provide very detailed descriptions of life "on the other side," and she even includes pictures and diagrams of that place.

Browne wrote about the use of a hovercraft on "the other side." She explained her belief that this vehicle is available to provide a spirit tremendous freedom. Her theory is comforting—and as plausible as any other explanation about what happens after the death of the body.

Kris and Sally talked about what fun it would be to drive and travel in such a craft. Kris could go anywhere anytime in

her hovercraft. She smiled when she talked about it. They
enjoyed talking about life "on the other side," and Kris
derived much pleasure sharing her thoughts about what it
would be like zooming around in her hovercraft.

Browne's books gave them a framework to describe some
of the unusual experiences they shared during the last
months of Kris's life. Driving back before dawn from a
favorite restaurant in Cheyenne, Wyoming, they enjoyed
watching the sunrise. One day in November on that familiar
road, they both saw a sunrise that was different from anything
they'd seen before.

Sally said, "The sky seemed huge—infinite in size both
horizontally and vertically. The hues of the colors filled the
whole sky. The vision we saw had a surreal quality, and it was
mesmerizing. An artist couldn't have painted that. Not even a
computer could have created what we saw. The colors were
vibrant, intense and more fantastic than words can describe.
This vision had an other-worldly quality, and we were both
awe-struck. Neither of us said anything because there were no
words to describe the experience. Both of us knew we were
watching a glimpse of the other side."

That experience was comforting to Sally. She explained
that seeing that vision reassured her that Kris was going to a
beautiful place. After the colors faded into ordinary daylight,
they talked about "the other side" and how welcoming it
would be for Kris.

Kris and I had numerous discussions about what happens
right after death because that was what scared her. Because
her energy was waning, we focused our discussions on the
areas that were most important to her. If she'd expressed

concerns or fears about other parts of the process, we would have talked more about them.

Even though she didn't bring up any concerns about the moment of death or the time leading up to her death, I thought it was important to explore those areas with her. I wanted to be sure we were not omitting anything that would help her to have the "good death" that was important to her. I looked for simple, practical guidelines for helping someone die well and couldn't find them. Following my instincts, I directed Kris to a story about someone else's death.

Kris had read Mitch Albom's wonderful little book *Tuesdays with Morrie* many years ago. This story describes the author's weekly visits with one of his former college professors in the last months of the older man's life. The professor, Morrie, was dying from ALS (amyotrophic lateral sclerosis, also known as Lou Gehrig's disease). A movie, based on the book, was also available. I encouraged Kris and Sally to watch the movie together and talk about it. Watching the movie helped Kris and Sally become more realistic about Kris's declining health and increasing limitations.

Kris told me, "Watching the scene where he says he knows the day will come when he can no longer wipe himself after using the toilet was a good reality hit. It's good for me to prepare myself for that."

I continued my search for resources to help Kris create the dying experience she wanted. My self-directed study led me to Sounds True, a publishing company which disseminates interfaith wisdom through the voices of leading authors, teachers and experts of our times. In their catalogue

I found the series of six audiotapes *Being With Dying* by
Joan Halifax. (Available through Amazon.com)
Tape #2 includes the following nine contemplations on
dying:

1. Death is inevitable.
2. Our life span is decreasing continuously.
3. Death will come whether or not we are prepared for it.
4. Human life expectancy is uncertain.
5. There are many causes of death.
6. The human body is fragile and vulnerable.
7. At the time of death our material resources are not of
   use to us.
8. Our loved ones cannot keep us from death.
9. Our own body cannot help us at the time of our death.

I lent Kris this tape when she expressed fears about
spending her money. She never spoke about the tape directly,
but later she quoted some of the contemplations, especially
"at the time of death our material resources are not of use to
us." It seemed that contemplating these nine statements was
useful to Kris.

Tape #6 includes a guided *phowa* practice from the
Buddhist tradition. Because it speaks of dying "a good and
peaceful death," I transcribed the prayer and gave Kris a
copy. After she died, I found it in her file folder marked
"Important Papers."

Halifax introduces the *phowa* prayer by saying, "The
purpose of the following prayer is to realize the pure nature
of the mind."

Through your blessing, grace and guidance,
Through the power of the light that streams
from you,
May all my negative karma, destructive emotions,
obscurations and blockages be purified
and removed,
May I know myself forgiven for all the harm
I have thought and done,
May I accomplish this profound practice
of phowa,
And die a good and peaceful death,
And through the triumph of my death,
May I be able to benefit all other beings
living or dead.

▲   ▲   ▲

Halifax closes the exercise by saying, "Remember that
you do this practice for your own liberation and to benefit
all beings."

Tape #6 also includes a powerful exercise: Halifax
provides specific directions on how to practice dying. By the
time I did this exercise, Kris was too ill to participate. When
I first heard the suggestion to practice dying it seemed
strange, and I felt resistant to doing the exercise. But I
thought about how valuable it is to practice childbirth and
realized it could be just as valuable to practice leaving this
world. I diligently followed the instructions lying on the floor
in the privacy of my living room.

Going through the practice of dying was empowering. I felt a sense of calm as I listened to the voice on the tape guiding me to focus on my breath. Going through this process took away the fear and mystery of death. The experience made me more comfortable talking with Kris about how she could relax her body and follow the light.

Shortly after I'd listened to the sixth tape, Kris talked about her fear of getting lost after the moment of death. One of her biggest fears was that after she died, she would see someone she wanted to avoid. I thought about what I'd learned on the tapes, and I helped her practice "going to the light."

I said to her, "Kris, at the moment of your death your only job will be to follow the light. I will guide you with my words so you can practice. Close your eyes and let your whole body relax. Imagine your life force leaving your body. Your spirit is free now. Imagine that you can see a beautiful, bright light. It is easy to follow the light. With your eyes closed, keep looking at the light, and you will go toward it. You are safe now. Follow the light."

As she practiced following the light, a slight smile came to her face, and a visible sense of peace came to her body. I could see the tension in her body dissipate. Her breathing became less labored.

6

BEING
REMEMBERED

K ris continued to be mobile getting around with a
walker, going to restaurants and stores and having
meaningful visits with people at her home. I wanted to be
sure we talked about all the important things while her mind
was still clear. My fear was that her cancer would spread to
her brain, and she would be unable to carry on conversations.

That never happened, but a thought kept worrying me,
"What if there's something really important to talk about and
I don't think of it until it's too late?"

I had read about the importance of asking people who
are dying how they want to be remembered. I realized that
even though I'd known Kris for many years, I didn't know
how she wanted to be remembered. It had never occurred to
me to ask Kris that question.

At her house one snowy morning I asked, "Kris, tell me
how you want to be remembered."

She wasn't sure how to answer. "Let me think about it, and I'll write some things," she said.

For a while, every few days I asked her that question in some form. "Kris, how do you want people to think of you after you're gone?"

"I'll think about that," she said again.

I wondered if she was avoiding the topic or if she just needed more time.

About two weeks later when I came to Kris's home, she handed me a piece of paper and said, "These are the ways I want to be remembered."

She wrote:

- A generous person with gifts, ideas, knowledge and humor
- Creatively helpful to self and others
- Finding peace with spirituality
- Giving away all her earthly gifts to benefit others
- Kind and compassionate

I knew she liked having the list because she included it in her folder for her memorial service. She also used this description of herself in her obituary. Once I knew how Kris wanted to be remembered, I could acknowledge these attributes in her whenever I saw them.

7

THE LAST
GIFTS

The winter holiday season arrived seven months after Kris's diagnosis. She and Sally decided to skip their usual Christmas traditions. They were stressed enough by the activities of daily life without adding to their routine. Skipping their usual holiday traditions proved to be a good decision for both of them.

For many years Kris and I had exchanged little gifts for the holidays and for birthdays. I wanted to give Kris a meaningful present for her last Christmas, and I also wanted to find something special for her birthday. I had no idea what those gifts would be. It was difficult to think of an appropriate gift for this stage of her life. At the same time, I didn't want to treat her as if she had already died. I went to our local greeting card shop but had no success finding a suitable card either for Christmas or for Kris's upcoming birthday.

As a friend lamented, "They don't make cards for the last Christmas of your life or your last birthday."

My dilemma for the holidays was solved when I learned about Heifer International. This non-profit organization—www.heifer.org—works to help end world hunger and poverty through self-reliance and sustainability. Heifer provides gifts of animals to needy families worldwide and ensures rigorous training for their recipients. The program has a unique opportunity for those in poverty to help others and themselves. All recipients agree to pass on their training and skills, and one or more of the animals' offspring to another family in need.

Heifer sent Kris a card letting her know I'd given a gift in her honor. I chose this gift because it was consistent with her values of being creative and generous to others. I never knew how she responded to the gift. She was too ill for either of us to think about thank you notes.

In March, only a month before Kris died, I found the book *Life Lessons* by Elisabeth Kübler-Ross and David Kessler. I gave it to Kris as a birthday present and thought I might read it to her during my visits. By that time, ten months after her diagnosis, Kris was spending many daytime hours in bed. She was heavily medicated to manage her pain, which meant she spent many hours sleeping during the day.

Sometimes when I came to her home she wanted to talk. Other times she dozed, although I knew she appreciated my presence because she smiled and nodded when I sat with her and held her hand.

I gave her the book as a birthday present as soon as I found it—even though it was four weeks before her birthday (and four weeks before she died). Each of the fourteen chapters addresses a different topic. If I'd had the book sooner, I would have structured some of my conversations with Kris around those topics. When she was awake and unable to carry on a conversation, I asked her if she wanted me to read to her. Since she nodded yes, I read to her starting with the chapter on Love. Later, I read aloud to her the chapter on Surrender.

In retrospect, I realized there were various things, such as the Heifer present and reading aloud, to which I never knew her response. At the time, I didn't think to ask. I know that we were all doing the best we could and that was good enough.

I believed what Kris said many times, "It will all happen exactly as it's supposed to happen."

In the last few weeks of her life, there were times when I sat with her quietly and neither of us talked. As I held her hand, I focused my mind on her positive attributes and how she wanted to be remembered. Since I knew that hearing is the last sense to go, sometimes I talked to Kris, filling the silence with positive, loving words.

For example, I told her how successful her life had been, "I admire you so much for staying committed to your path of personal growth. You are remarkable for facing demons from your past and working through indescribably painful feelings. You do such an incredible job of living a life of honesty and integrity. I like it that I can trust you completely. You are always true to your word. I can count on you to do what you say. I love it that you're always learning new things."

During those times I felt a life-affirming, palpable energy in the room. It didn't matter that she wasn't able to respond.

8

A PSYCHIC
READING

About six weeks before she died, Kris asked me to
schedule a session with a psychic. She wanted me to ask
two questions.

- What else is important for Kris to do while she's still here?
- How much longer does she have here?

I thought about how people's spiritual beliefs influence
their experience. I know in this area there is no such thing
as right or wrong. There is not one ultimate truth. Working
with Kris—including taking her questions to a psychic—
reinforced my desire to support her in any beliefs that gave
her comfort and peace during this transition.

When psychics do readings, they typically close their eyes
and contact "spiritual entities" who give advice for the clients
seeking help. These psychic readings may also be called

"intuitive readings." The person doing the reading is considered a "medium" who channels information from the spirit world to those of us on earth.

When clients are skeptical about the process, it is common for spiritual entities to provide highly personal, confidential information to the client through the medium. Since the information couldn't have been known by the person channeling the message, this can be startling to the client and builds belief in the process. Kris believed in the work of psychics and had consulted with several over the years. Her request was based on her past positive experiences.

I took copious notes as the psychic channeled responses to Kris's questions. After I shared the message with Kris, she didn't say anything, but I could see her body relax. I could tell she found the information helpful and meaningful. The message the psychic channeled for Kris follows:

This choice of disease, length of time and Kris still being active makes it possible for her to do a whole lifetime in this last time. She came in to do a healing journey. She's packing it into this whole dying process. The most important task for Kris during this period of time is for her to learn to receive. To trust and to focus on what is being given, not on what isn't being given. She has all the right people around her. The illness allows her to receive.

She is doing a lot in a short time. A lot of good is coming her way, and she is learning to accept love and care, allowing someone to hold her hand. The more she believes she deserves it, the more healing she will have. She is doing by receiving. Everything comes back to love.

She is doing five years in ten days. What she can do in the next ten days is like five years in another lifetime.

Encourage her to relax, relax inside. Let the sun shine on you (Judy). You don't have to prepare, don't have to do anything. Just relax. The universe and the angels around her will take care of her. There is healing in having the disease and dying. Remember she is eternal. Everything she gains now will go with her. Now is about receiving.

If there are other things to do with the outer world, she'll think of them. It's like she's gotten her doctorate and now her post-doctoral work is to accept and receive love and integrate it. It can be from people, animals and anything of the earth—rocks, trees. Whatever ounce she takes in, every ounce is worth a gallon of accepting and letting it in. This is about love.

She's done a lot in the living stage. This is the receiving stage. She is already perfect. She is deserving. What is coming for her is so much brightness. She's also being of service to others now when she lets others love her.

In the dying is healing. Every breath she takes is a sacred breath. Every part of her is with the divine. She can realize the divine is throughout her. She is sacred now. Every breath she takes is Spirit going through her. She is worthy of love now.

At the moment of death, she'll be greeted and helped to a comfortable, nurturing healing place to finish the healing that hasn't happened yet. She will follow the light and be exactly where she is supposed to be. If she sees anyone or anything she doesn't want to see, all she needs to do is say "no" to that, turn away and follow the light.

Kris is meant to be leaving here before long. Can't tell the amount of time it will take. That is between her and Spirit. It will be when it is right for her.

9

WRITING THE OBITUARY

I asked Kris to write a first draft of her obituary. I told her, "This will be a working copy. It's not supposed to be perfect. Nobody's going to see this first copy except us, so write whatever you want. Don't be concerned with how others will respond. We'll think about that later."

Kris read other people's obituaries in the newspaper and noticed some she liked and others she didn't. Some people had obviously thought about what was written and had beautifully articulated obituaries. And with others, it was obvious that they were put together hastily and gave only basic facts about the deceased's life.

I told Kris about a friend whom I cared about deeply although I had lost touch with her. One morning, about a year before Kris's diagnosis, I was sitting at my breakfast table reading the newspaper. As I turned the page, I saw my friend's picture and read her obituary. She had died of cancer at the age of forty-seven.

I was shocked and traumatized to learn of her death in that way. I hadn't even known she was ill. I read and re-read her obituary, grateful that it was long and detailed, giving me a summary of her life. She included specifics from her childhood, her teen years, her education, her career and her romantic life.

Reading her obituary was like listening to someone tell me about my friend. Each time I read it, I learned more about her, and I felt as if I had just spent time with her. It was beautifully written, focusing on many happy, positive times of her life.

I felt comforted as I read my friend's obituary over and over again while looking at her photograph. I was glad to read where and when the memorial service would be so I could attend. As I talked with other people at the service, I learned about the events of her last year and that she had wanted to keep her illness a secret.

The way I learned about her death—suddenly and without warning—affected me deeply. For the first time, I realized how important an obituary could be for the people who are still alive.

When I came home from that memorial service, I wrote my own obituary. As I imagined myself close to death, I felt deep sadness about the loss of my future. I also felt tremendous grief at the thought of leaving my loved ones. And I imagined the grief they would feel if I died. It was one of the saddest times I have ever experienced.

With tears streaming down my face, I sat at the computer and reviewed my life. I wrote my obituary, sharing highlights from various stages of my life. It made me happy to create a

picture of myself so others would know me better. I imagined
people smiling as they learned more about me. Writing my
obituary was cathartic, and I felt satisfied when I finished. I
was pleased that people would remember me the way I
wanted to be known. I felt reassured to have control of what
was written and how it was presented.

I left a few blanks, knowing I will probably revise it in
the years to come. I put a copy of it with my will and told
my loved ones I had written my obituary. Following is what
I wrote:

Judy K. Underwood, partner, mom, grandma, daughter,
sister, aunt, niece, cousin, friend, psychotherapist, life
coach, author, speaker and role model died DAY,
DATE, of CAUSE. She was AGE. She was at home
surrounded by her family and others who loved her.

All who knew Judy are invited to attend a
memorial gathering at TIME, PLACE.

She grew up in Belleville, New Jersey, living with
both of her parents, her maternal grandparents and
two sisters. She was the middle of three girls. Judy was
a beautiful person both inside and out. In 1964, she
was crowned Miss Cherry Blossom of Belleville and
went on to win First Runner Up in the Miss Essex
County beauty pageant. She was a rebellious teenager,
enjoying parties and running around with boyfriends.

The stories about Judy reflect her Aries nature.
She was born before her due date and did most
things sooner than expected. She whizzed through
Douglass College, New Brunswick, New Jersey, in

three years, earning a bachelor's degree in Speech
Pathology in 1966. She chose her major so she could
combine a career with motherhood, which was a
common practice for women at that time. She earned
her master's degree in the same field in 1967 at Kean
University, Union, New Jersey.

Judy enjoyed swimming and loved the outdoors.
In the summers while she was a student, she was a life
guard at a nursing school. After she got her master's
degree, she worked as a speech and language
pathologist at Mountainside Hospital, Montclair,
New Jersey. She worked in a small school for the
deaf in the southern part of the state and later as an
administrator for the Tri-County Easter Seals Society
in southern New Jersey.

In the spirit of adventure, she moved "out west"
and earned her Ph.D. in Communication Disorders
at the age of twenty-seven from the University of
Denver. She taught at the University of Northern
Colorado, Greeley, Colorado, for ten years from
1972–1982. Her classes in speech and language
pathology were popular with undergraduate and
graduate students. Her work in clinical supervision
received national recognition. She was promoted to
full professor and was elected Chairperson of the
Faculty Senate. During that time, she published
scholarly papers and presented research findings at
national and international conferences.

Her first marriage was at the age of nineteen. After
two years, she went to Reno, Nevada, to get divorced,

as was the custom in the 1960s. She married again at age twenty-two and during this thirteen-year marriage gave birth to her beloved daughter, Danya. After a second divorce, Judy found her life partner, Dr. Pamela Gaynor. They created a non-traditional life together that was a model for many other women. Their love and support will be carried forward into the future.

In 1982, Judy made a career change and became a psychotherapist. She joined Pam's psychotherapy practice of Centennial Center for Human Services. Over the years, Judy became well-known and highly regarded for her ability to combine caring and competence. Her clients came from Denver, Greeley, Boulder and Wyoming, as well as Fort Collins. In 1999, she became certified as an executive and life coach and worked with clients from all over the country by phone. She was passionate about helping people live happier, healthier lives.

After coaching a terminally ill client through the last eleven months of her life, Judy wrote and published the book *Dying: Finding Comfort and Guidance in a Story of a Peaceful Passing*. She wanted others to know how to help their loved ones achieve peace at the end of life.

Judy loved being a mother and devoted a great deal of energy to being a parent. She was masterful at combining career with motherhood.

She lived a rich, full life. She traveled to many places in the world, enjoyed spending time with Pam, dancing, doing yoga, going to the gym, reading, riding her bike, exploring past lives, attending reunions with her high school friends the Pi Gamma Sigmas, and being a lifelong learner. Prior to becoming a mother, she jumped out of an airplane and enjoyed the thrill of skydiving.

She dreamed of becoming a philanthropist and was dedicated to making the world a more friendly and accepting place for everyone. She contributed regularly to organizations and charities that were close to her heart. She was a founding contributor to the Holocaust Museum in Washington, D.C., and a staunch supporter of the pro-choice movement.

Judy's mission was to be a role-model for younger women. Clearly, she succeeded.

Judy is survived by _____.

Please honor Judy's memory by making contributions to NAME AND ADDRESS.

▲ ▲ ▲

I sat at the computer working on my obituary late into the night. I lost all sense of time and experienced a range of emotions while I worked. By the end, I was both exhausted and exhilarated. I had not thought of some of the things that occurred in my life for years. Writing the obituary helped me remember important, formative times in my life. I also felt a deeper connection to the many people I loved. The words explain how I want to be remembered. The words also deepened my resolve always to live in love.

I knew Kris would gain the same feelings. Even though Kris knew it was important for her to write her own obituary, she procrastinated. I broached the topic many times in a gentle way. I wasn't sure how much time we had left, and I didn't want to wait until it was too late. Each time I brought up the idea, she said she was "thinking about it." Once she said, "it's too soon."

I knew how sad it was for me to write my obituary. I assumed writing it would be even harder for her because it would make her face the reality of her impending death.

She didn't mind that I prodded her. She wanted to decide what information would be included and how she would portray herself.

The obituary is an important final document. Information included not only serves as a reminder of a life to loved ones, it also provides a historical record that might be referenced in the future.

Funeral homes pay a lot of attention to the obituary. We didn't know ahead of time that the funeral home would give Sally laminated copies of the obituary to keep and distribute. The funeral home also surprised us with copies of the obituary that they made into bookmarks for us to have as keepsakes.

According to Furman and McNaab, authors of *The Dying Time,* "The purpose of the obituary is to notify the public of the passing of your loved one and to give honor to the deceased by relating some of his [or her] personal accomplishments in life. Many people also retain a copy of the obituary as a memento."

Although an obituary is not a requirement, I knew Kris wanted an announcement in the local newspaper and in her hometown paper. The funeral home contacted both newspapers and let us know the cost and the guidelines for each publication. I was unaware that many newspapers charge a significant fee to publish an obituary or death notice. It was helpful to contact the papers ahead of time to inquire about the charges. We might have published a shorter version in the newspapers and handed out a longer version to friends and family at the service. Obituaries can be placed in any newspaper. Specialty publications such as alumni magazines and trade journals also publish obituaries.

Six months after her diagnosis, Kris said she was ready to work on her obituary. I gave Kris a copy of my obituary as a model and explained that the experience of writing it made me incredibly sad, but also brought me a deep feeling of satisfaction. She understood that writing her own obituary would help her move through her grief.

One fall morning when I came to her home, she handed me her rough draft. She asked for feedback, and together we made a few minor changes. Here is her final draft:

> Kristie M. (Kris) Rempfer, 57, of Fort Collins, died DATE, peacefully at home in Fort Collins from complications of cancer. She was surrounded with love and caring from many of the special people in her life.
>
> A memorial service will be at TIME, at PLACE WITH ADDRESS. NAME will officiate. Kris has requested attendees dress casually in bright celebratory colors. Jeans are welcome.
>
> Kris was born April 14, 1947, in Rapid City, SD. Her childhood years were spent living in many different towns in South Dakota.

In grade school and high school, Kris was an accomplished musician. During her eighth grade year, she was the featured soloist on her cornet with the Le Mars, Iowa, high school orchestra. Kris won many high musical rankings as a soloist.

As a young adult, Kris worked for the Forest Service as an organization development specialist and lived on both coasts for a number of years.

In 1978, Kris moved to Denver and earned her bachelor of arts degree in human services with an emphasis on drugs, alcohol and other addictive behaviors, from Metropolitan State College.

It was in Denver in 1980 that Kris met her soulmate, Sally Juday. Kris and Sally spent many years with a business in remodeling and real estate investing and lived a full, loving life with each other.

Kris lived her life with gusto. She had many adventures and travels. She lived on a sailboat in both Northern and Southern California and spent many weeks camping on the Baja peninsula and riding her motorcycle.

She was an avid sportswoman, participating in softball, flag football, rugby, hiking, bicycling and racquet sports. In midlife, she took up golf and loved playing it with Sally.

The friends and relatives who shared her life will always remember her as a gentle soul whose chosen path touched many people in immeasurable ways. She was a kind and compassionate person who was generous with gifts, ideas, knowledge and humor. She was creatively helpful to self and others. At the end of her life, she found peace with spirituality and gave away her earthly belongings to benefit others.

She is survived by Sally Juday, her lifetime partner; special mentor, Dr. Judy Underwood; her loving sister, JoAnne Amsden; her older sister, Nancy Hunsley; and her mother, Gertrude Rempfer; along with several nieces and nephews. She was preceded in death by her father, Alvin; and brother, Mark.

In lieu of flowers, memorial contributions may be made to Hospice of Larimer County, Turning Point or the Larimer Humane Society in care of NAME & ADDRESS OF FUNERAL HOME.

Visit WEBSITE to view an online obituary and sign a guest book.

▲ ▲ ▲

Kris had a sense of accomplishment from completing this task. She didn't want to explain her feelings any further. She didn't say much about her experience writing her obituary.

We talked about possible reactions loved ones might have to things she had written. She made a few changes and felt strongly about not making other changes based on others' sensitivities. She was happy with the obituary she had written and asked us to fill in the blanks after her death.

Writing an obituary is a strange and unfamiliar experience. For each of us it was cathartic. Both Kris and I gained important perspectives on our accomplishments, our loved ones, our losses and our most memorable experiences. Kris—who was near death—recognized very quickly that her life comprised a grand experience. My experience emphasized the preciousness of life's every moment.

10

HOSPICE

There were many reasons that I figured it would be useful to contact our local Hospice program to learn what it offered. I wanted Kris and Sally to know what resources were available. That way they could make informed decisions based on facts instead of preconceived ideas. I wanted them to talk with Hospice workers.

I thought of a friend who had told me her family didn't want to contact Hospice when her mother was dying. They thought it would mean they were giving up. After her mother's death, she had tears in her eyes as she told me how badly they needed help and didn't know where to turn. Unfortunately, many people believe that contacting Hospice means defeat. In my experience with Kris, I learned that contacting Hospice means making a wise choice to get valuable help during a very difficult time.

Elisabeth Kübler-Ross, M.D., in *The Wheel of Life: A Memoir of Living and Dying*, wrote about her experience as a physician working with terminally ill patients and teaching medical and theology students. She believed, "Death was a part of life, the most important part of life."

She wrote that she received little support from her colleagues. "In a physician's mind, death meant something else. It meant failure. I could not help but observe how everybody at the hospital avoided the subject of death.... Physicians who were brilliant at prolonging life did not understand death was a part of it."

I didn't want Kris to feel like a failure for dying. Everyone dies. If Kris thought of dying as a part of living, she could acknowledge her own mortality and plan for a satisfying, meaningful transition. Equating death with failure would prevent her from achieving inner peace before she died. Borrowing some help from the Hospice model, we talked about death as a completion, a graduation from life.

Initially, Kris and Sally didn't want to contact Hospice. Their resistance seemed related to not wanting to think about Kris's impending death and worrying about finances.

We learned that Hospice is for people who are in the last six months of life. Kris said, "but what if I live for another year or two?"

I told her, "You're right, you might live another year or two. We have no way to know for sure. Either the doctors don't know or they have a good idea and don't want to tell you. In any case, it can't hurt to go to Hospice and talk with them. If Hospice thinks you're not eligible, they'll tell you. If it doesn't feel right to you, or you don't like what you see or hear there, you don't have to sign up. I'll go with you if you want. Let's just make an appointment and learn more about what's possible. Think of it as a research project."

Framing Hospice as something to learn about made it possible for Kris and Sally to agree to meet with the local program workers. The three of us made an appointment with the person in charge of intake.

We found the meeting very useful. It was good to hear that the goal of Hospice is not to help a person find a cure. The focus of Hospice was clearly:

- to help Kris do whatever was important to her while she was still alive
- to prevent her from suffering

The administrator told us many useful things that we didn't know. She let us know about the personnel at Hospice and the services they provide. These are the services that were available from Hospice for Kris and her loved ones:

- **Nurse**—made weekly home visits for physical assessment and communicated directly with the oncologist so Kris didn't have to go to the doctor's office. The nurse drew blood at home and had medicine delivered. Numerous medicines were available to alleviate pain and the various physical problems that accompany a terminal illness. The nurse also arranged for home healthcare equipment such as a walker, wheelchair, shower bench, hospital bed and other physical aids when needed.
- **Social Worker**—provided counseling for Kris, Sally and loved ones.

- **Nurse's Aides**—helped with bathing and eating.
- **Music Therapist**—made home visits and played music.
- **Chaplain**—an interdenominational spiritual advisor made home visits. This person's job is to support and encourage people's beliefs, not to recruit or tell anyone what to believe.
- **Medical Director**—an M.D. who made home visits as necessary.
- **Volunteers**—mostly women who spent time with Kris and helped with chores.
- **Grief Support Groups**—available for a patient's loved ones. Hospice promises to support the family of a loved one for thirteen months following the death. The level of support varies depending on the need and receptivity of the family, as well as the available resources of a particular Hospice. For the year following Kris's death, Sally received encouraging mailings. She also attended a comforting eight-week grief support group and a meaningful yearly memorial service.
- **Support Groups for Caregivers**—provided an opportunity to talk with others in a similar situation.

I left the meeting feeling confident that Hospice would be a valuable resource to help Kris fulfill her wish of dying "a good death." What I didn't realize until later was how valuable Hospice would be to all of us. We were fortunate that Hospice workers helped us for nine months.

Hospice accepts patients with a doctor's referral. In 2004, the year Kris died, her medical insurance covered a maximum of $8200 or nine months of care, whichever came first. We learned most people contacted Hospice when it was too late to use many of its services.

Even though the initial meeting at Hospice was emotional for Kris and Sally, both of them were pleased that I pushed them to that meeting early in the process. The visit gave them time to think about what was said and their options. Talking with actual Hospice workers made the prospect of using the service much less frightening. Going to the Hospice building was a positive experience and helped Kris feel more in control of her life—and death. We visited their lending library and borrowed some books.

Soon after the visit and two months after her diagnosis, Kris signed up with the local program. Her oncologist made the necessary referral. Because Kris was still functioning well, it allowed her to get involved with Hospice in a gradual way. Initially, she and Sally met with a counselor once every few weeks. Later, he came more often. They met with a nurse once a week and built more and more trust with each visit.

Having time to build relationships with the Hospice workers enhanced the quality of Kris's life and contributed to effective pain management. With the help of the Hospice nurse, Kris experienced very little pain. The nurse had an opportunity to know Kris over time and consequently did a better job adjusting her medicines when needed. She also made excellent recommendations for home health aids, which made Kris's life easier (I'll explain more about home health aids in Chapter 17).

We learned that the local Hospice program operates a wing in one of the local hospitals that could be used if needed. It was comforting to know that if Kris had a medical emergency, or for some other reason couldn't be cared for at home, she could be moved to the Hospice wing.

Basically, the Hospice philosophy says this—when people are dying they should have the care they need. No one should die alone, and no one should die in pain. For some people that means dying at home; for others dying in a Hospice facility is better. There is no right or wrong way to die. Each situation is different, and the optimal situation needs to be determined for each individual case.

We considered what resources were available and talked about both Kris's and Sally's needs and wants.

Kris loved music. As her health declined, it was harder for her to leave the house. About three months before she died, Kris requested a visit from the Hospice music therapist. A woman came to their home and played the flute for about forty-five minutes. The music was beautiful and peaceful. The melodies helped Kris relax and travel to far off places in her mind. She asked for the music therapist once more before she died.

The Hospice director assured us that if Kris lived longer than six months she would not be turned away in the last part of her life because of money. In the end, Kris's medical insurance paid for all of her Hospice care. The Hospice billing department did an excellent job dealing with the insurance company. When we were told the last month of Hospice care wouldn't be covered by insurance, Sally paid that bill. Over a year later, Sally got a reimbursement check from Hospice. Thanks to the diligence of the Hospice billing department, the insurance company finally paid for Kris's last month of care.

After Kris's death, Sally attended a Hospice Bereavement Support Group and found the experience comforting. She also participated in the Hospice Annual Memorial Service where she read the following poem published in the *Gates of Prayer: Reform Judaism Prayerbook.*

We Remember Them
By Rabbi Sylvan Kamens

If life is sacred it should not be allowed to perish.
True, the body will return to dust, but the
remembrance of life should continue.
We are not dead until we are forgotten.

*At the rising sun and at its going down we
remember them.*

*At the blowing of the wind and in the chill of
winter we remember them.*

*At the opening of the buds and in the rebirth of spring
we remember them.*

*At the blueness of the skies and in the warmth of
summer we remember them.*

*At the rustling of the leaves and in the beauty of
autumn we remember them.*

*At the beginning of the year and when it ends we
remember them.*

*As long as we live, they too will live; for they are now
a part of us as we remember them.*

*When we are weary and in need of strength we
remember them.*

*When we are lost and sick at heart we
remember them.*

*When we have decisions that are difficult to
make we remember them.*

*When we have joy we crave to share we
remember them.*

*When we have achievements that are based
on theirs we remember them.*

For as long as we live, they too will live,

*For they are now a part of us, as we
remember them.*

▲   ▲   ▲

Kris, Sally and I all felt tremendous gratitude for Hospice
and were glad we didn't delay contacting them. Hospice is
truly one of the most wonderful, loving programs ever
developed.

11

EATING &
WELLNESS HABITS

When Kris learned she had an illness for which there was no cure, one of the hardest things for her was to change her mindset about eating. Kris and Sally usually ate healthy foods and paid close attention to their diets. They also ate most of their meals in familiar restaurants at specific times.

I talked with Kris about how priorities, responsibilities and obligations naturally change at the end of life. Although she agreed this was true, it remained tremendously important to her to be at her favorite restaurant for breakfast when it opened at 6 a.m. She couldn't imagine that changing.

Both Kris and Sally had to retrain their minds to think differently about food and Kris's eating patterns. Certain things that mattered in the past didn't matter anymore.

Sally had to stop encouraging Kris to eat when she lost interest in food. When a certain food stopped tasting good to her, it was eliminated. It wasn't necessary to search for other things that tasted good to her. Adequate nutrition is a priority for people who are healthy. Nutrition is also a priority for people who are ill and getting better. This is not true for people who are dying. Someone who is dying doesn't need to eat.

Just as Kris needed to change her mindset about her eating patterns, she needed to change the way she thought about her routine health care. Before her cancer diagnosis, Kris took pride in her physical health and rarely got sick. Other than smoking, she lived a healthy lifestyle and focused on maintaining wellness.

When Kris looked at her calendar and saw her routine dental appointment she said, "I have a dental appointment in two weeks."

I knew she had a phobia about going to the dentist and these appointments caused her great anxiety. Even routine dental cleanings caused her distress.

I told her, "You know, you don't have to keep your appointment."

She said, "I always go to the dentist every six months."

I took her hand in mine and looked into her eyes as I replied, "Kris," I said, "You can go, if you want to. And this time, it would be OK not to go. Since we know you don't have too much time left here, it's really up to you if you keep this appointment or not. Your teeth and mouth aren't hurting or having any problem. Getting your teeth cleaned is one of those things that you do to keep your mouth healthy for the long term. It's not important to do that now for health reasons. If you want to do it now for any reason, you can do it. It's totally your choice."

Kris gave me a blank look. Not keeping her regular appointments was a foreign idea to her. I made the same point using different words.

I said, "Kris, I just don't want you to go to the dentist because you think you should, or because it's in your calendar, or because you've already made the appointment. I want you to make a conscious choice about whether it's important to you or not at this time of your life. Things are different now, and you can make different choices. It's OK to cancel the appointment if you don't want to go."

This was one of many times I said to her, "The rules are different now." When someone is dying the rules change, whether they are about diet, exercise or regular health care appointments.

Kris cancelled her dental appointment. This was when she started using the word "bittersweet" to describe situations. The description was fitting.

Together, the three of us created *Three Rules For Kris*. Sally and I needed frequent reminders of these rules as much as Kris did. We knew it was important for her well-being to change our thinking about her eating and health care routine. Here are the three rules:

1. It's OK not to eat

We told Kris, "You should do exactly what you want about food. You should not be encouraged or cajoled to eat if you aren't interested."

When someone is dying, the body shuts down and cannot digest food properly. If we pushed Kris to eat, we would be doing harm. Our actions would lead to her discomfort from constipation. We were not starving her; we were respecting the natural shutting down of her body.

2. It's OK to eat whatever you want whenever you want

We said to Kris, "Portion size can be as tiny as you want. Nutritional information and balanced diets don't matter anymore." There were many times we needed to remind ourselves of this rule because it wasn't easy to shift our usual way of thinking.

Kris was hypoglycemic and typically avoided sugar. In the last months of her life she went on a dessert eating spree, choosing a different treat each day. Her favorite dessert was mud pie. This process brought her great joy. In the last weeks of her life, her primary food choice was no-sugar-added ice cream.

As Kris got closer to death, she became less interested in food. We knew she would need to stop eating when she was ready to die. We told her and reminded ourselves, "It's OK to eat, and it's OK to stop eating. Continuing to eat may prolong your life. When you're ready to die, you'll stop eating and that's OK."

3. It's OK to think short-term instead of long-term

Kris was disciplined about taking care of her health. She had yearly medical check ups, mammograms, and had her teeth cleaned regularly. She was startled to realize she could cancel all her routine medical appointments. This gave her the opportunity to save her limited time and energy for other things that were more important to her and gave her pleasure.

Kris smoked for the major part of her life and thought about quitting many times. When she learned she was dying, she realized there were other things she wanted to make a higher priority than trying, again, to quit smoking. Although she stopped working to overcome her addiction, she still insisted on going outside to smoke. It was a matter of pride to her not to smoke in their home.

When smoking became difficult because of her lack of energy and mobility, she considered a nicotine patch or nicotine gum. These might have been useful to her although she never tried them.

Whenever she brought up the topic of smoking, she said, "I know that one day I'll lose interest in smoking and stop." In fact, that happened two days before she died.

12

DYING AT HOME

Shortly after Kris enrolled in the Hospice program, I realized I didn't know if she wanted to die at home or in the hospital. I also didn't know Sally's preference.

In a straightforward manner I asked, "Kris, let's talk about where you want to die. Do you want to die at home or somewhere else? Tell me how you want it to be."

She answered right away without needing to think about it. "I want to die at home if possible. If not, I guess I would go to the hospital. We need to think about what's right for Sally, too."

I had no preconceived notion that one place would be better than another. I wanted to support Kris and Sally in whatever choices they made. Both of them agreed they would prefer for Kris to die at home. None of us really had any idea of the consequences of that decision or how much work that would be.

Initially, they thought everything would stay the same until Kris died. Because she had spent her whole life being fiercely independent and self-sufficient, we didn't consider the realities of the care she would need. We also didn't anticipate the enormous toll it would take on all of us. As Kris's health declined, she became more and more fatigued and less able to do even the simplest things for herself.

As we talked about dying at home, it became clear that there would be many advantages for Kris. She could have more control of her life and her death. She would be more comfortable in familiar surroundings and she could maintain her routines. She would continue to enjoy the company of her cats and have easy access to all her personal belongings. She would also be with Sally most of the time.

Sally wanted to be in their own home while she cared for Kris. She wanted to provide a warm, loving environment where Kris was surrounded by people she knew. Sally wanted to be physically close to Kris day and night. She wanted to be her primary caregiver and do all she could for her. She didn't want to spend long hours at the hospital, and she didn't want to spend her time driving back and forth. Neither of them wanted to deal with the staff and routines that go along with a hospital stay.

As Kris's health declined and she became more disabled, I realized the major disadvantage of dying at home was the lack of caregivers. While it was possible to arrange for helpers to come to their home, making the arrangements required a lot of time and energy. Sally's resistance to accept help from others also made a home death more challenging.

Sally knew she would be living in their home after Kris died. She felt peaceful about having Kris spend the end of her life there. She wanted to be with Kris when she died, and she wanted that to happen in their home.

Both agreed that if there were any emergencies that couldn't be handled at home, Kris would be taken to the Hospice wing at the hospital. Even though neither thought this would be necessary, it was important to have this agreement.

Here is a list of the difficult issues that we needed to consider as Kris's health declined:

Chores

Gradually Kris got weaker and weaker. She stopped doing chores around the house and asked Sally to take on her jobs. So, in addition to taking care of Kris, Sally assumed more of the household chores and responsibilities.

She took over all the tasks of caring for the cats, taking out the trash, washing the cars and straightening the house. Sally contacted service people regarding repairs and maintenance. She hired a service to clean the house once a month.

Even though Kris and Sally skipped most of their holiday activities, Kris wanted to keep the tradition of making their fructose pumpkin pies. She wanted to teach Sally how to make them. By mutual agreement, Kris supervised Sally's baking and, one last time, they enjoyed pumpkin pies together and gave them as gifts.

Caregivers

Sally believed that a "good partner" would do everything herself. It was obvious to me that everything that needed to be done was far too much for one person. Finally, when Sally was totally exhausted, she agreed that it was time to hire caregivers for the nights. By that time Kris was sleeping in a hospital bed in the living room. Having caregivers come in at night allowed Sally to sleep soundly and get some rest. This was necessary for the success of our plan for Kris to die at home.

Choosing a home death meant keeping numerous people committed to the process. We needed help from family, friends or hired caregivers twenty-four hours a day, seven days a week.

Personal Body Needs

As Kris's illness progressed, she gradually was able to do less and less for herself. She needed help washing, using the toilet, getting dressed and keeping track of and taking numerous medicines to manage her pain.

Medicines

Monitoring Kris's medicine was nearly a full-time job. Someone needed to get the correct pills and liquids four times a day and give them to her at the right times. Even though there were periods when she seemed stabilized on a particular regimen, as her illness progressed, changes were necessary. Medicines were added and deleted; doses were changed frequently. Monitoring Kris's medicines was a complex task. Sally found it helpful to keep a notebook where she wrote down all the changes as they occurred.

Kris died at home. But many times during the process Sally and I doubted our ability to perform all the necessary work. Dying anywhere is often a long, arduous process. Helping a loved one die at home is a noble goal, and the task is profoundly challenging.

13

ASKING FOR &
ACCEPTING HELP

When I agreed to help Kris "die a good death" I didn't know exactly what that meant, but I knew we would figure it out along the way. Because we already had a long-term therapy relationship, she turned to me for help with this part of her life, too. I didn't know the incredible amount of time and energy that would be required of me.

Our work together was very meaningful. I felt satisfied and fulfilled by what we accomplished.

Working with Kris was also stressful. Like many people who are thrust into the role of primary caregiver for a loved one who is dying, I was a novice in my new role with her. My only exposure to the death and dying process had been thirty-five years ago, when I read Elisabeth Kübler-Ross, M.D.'s, *On Death and Dying*. Published in 1969, it was the first book to address issues of death and dying directly. Much of the content was controversial, and it became a best seller that was translated into many languages. I read the book out of curiosity and didn't think about it again until Kris asked for my help.

After Kris's death I heard stories of people being overwhelmed and exhausted by the process of caring for terminally ill loved ones. I could relate to that experience. None of us knew how to help someone through this transition.

Caregivers often wonder if their loved one is getting the best possible care. In *Dying Well*, Byock describes the following guidelines for getting the best care for your loved one.

- a sense of responsibility to the dying person
- high expectations of the medical community and caregivers
- commitment to the process
- determination
- doctors, nurses, facilities and support services skilled in palliative care and aligned with the goals of the patient and family
- careful scrutiny rather than blind trust in professionals

If I'd known how hard it is to care for someone who is dying, I would have sought more help sooner. I wouldn't have felt so alone. Although there are advantages to dying at home, it can be extremely stressful for the caregivers who need to be on duty around the clock.

I had trouble finding enough hours in the day for everything I needed to accomplish. I spent twelve to fifteen hours a week either with Kris or coordinating her care. In addition to those hours, I thought about Kris from the moment I woke up to the time I went to sleep at night. I knew that once Kris died there would be no chance to correct mistakes. The life-and-death nature of the situation was compelling in a way I had never experienced.

Before Kris got sick, I had a busy practice with many days stretching from 8 a.m. until 8 p.m. Although my work with Kris was expanding, I continued to see all my other clients. I coped with the extra time demands by multi-tasking more than usual. During that period, I learned to use my cell phone while driving. I started my workday earlier in the morning and ended later in the evening. I eliminated some of my breaks between clients and shortened the time I allowed for meals. Every minute I saved was precious.

In my personal life, I had a long-term committed relationship to nurture and the other usual responsibilities of life. I knew it was imperative for my mental and physical health to continue my weekly yoga class, my regular workouts at the gym and keep my appointments with my life coach. I was grateful for the support of my partner, my daughter and my friends. They encouraged me and did their best not to make requests of me during that time.

At some points, I was barely holding things together. I came home at the end of each day exhausted. I woke up early every morning to start the routine all over again. When Kris needed me on weekends, I was there for her. When she didn't, I used the time for other areas of my life. During those eleven months, I only did chores and activities that were absolutely necessary. When my cat became ill and needed medical attention and when my washing machine broke down, those events became major catastrophes for me. I was already functioning at the outer edges of my limits. This was an emotional period for me with little time to process my feelings. My head and heart were always full. Because I was the professional caregiver, I thought I should be holding everything together with little trouble. In truth, I was struggling.

I remember one morning driving to Kris's house. I'd been traveling this route every day for so long the car seemed to drive itself. Suddenly, I was aware of a police officer behind me signaling me to pull over. As he approached my car, I burst into tears. I wasn't paying attention to anything other than my need to get to Kris's house by 8 a.m. Apparently, I'd been speeding.

Through my tears I said, "I'm sorry officer. I didn't realize I was going too fast. I have a client who's dying. I'm a psychotherapist, and I have to get there as soon as I can." I heard myself babbling, and I made myself stop talking. He took my license and registration and went back to his car.

My feelings were spinning out of control. I was scared. I wondered if he thought I was lying. Thoughts raced through my mind. Was he looking me up in the yellow pages? I chastised myself for having such thoughts. He returned and said something compassionate. Although his words didn't register, I was aware of his kind tone of voice. He told me to go on my way and watch my speed. I was grateful that he just gave me a warning. I took a few deep breaths and calmed myself the best I could. I gave myself permission to be late.

Both Kris and Sally had trouble admitting they needed help. They liked to do things themselves, and they hadn't socialized with others for many years. Being on the outside, I could see that getting help with basic activities would make life better for both of them.

They were no different from many people who are reluctant to ask for help. Especially when people are struggling with hardship—when they most need other people—they find it difficult to ask for help. Some people erroneously believe that they should be able to handle all problems themselves. They equate asking for help with being weak.

In fact, it takes strength to reach out and ask for help. Talking openly about a hardship and facing the truth about what's happening is a sign of strength, not weakness. Often the person who does not discuss hardships with others remains in a state of denial.

Actually, most people like being asked for help and are flattered when that happens. Reciprocal "give-and-take" makes relationships stronger. Businesses that offer help want to provide their services to others. People in the helping professions say their work makes their lives more meaningful.

When we ask for and receive help, we decrease the likelihood of burnout. When caregivers do too much, they downplay or ignore their own needs. This usually leads to anger and resentment. I wanted Sally to avoid resentment and burnout.

In Kris's presence I told Sally, "I've learned from Hospice that there are a number of companies in town that provide help to people in this kind of situation. You can hire someone to come in and stay with Kris while you go out. They can also help with chores."

Kris and Sally listened to my suggestions and responded politely that it was a good thing to know that help was available. But then they said, "We're OK for now" or "We can do it ourselves" or "We can manage."

The truth was that they were both totally exhausted. They were physically, mentally and spiritually drained.

They had many ways of resisting outside help—and I watched them get more and more exhausted. At various times, I mentioned ideas such as having someone else clean the house, hiring a personal chef to fill the freezer with healthy prepared meals, hiring a caregiver for certain hours of the day and taking Hospice up on their offer to have a volunteer come and help Sally with chores.

I also brought up the idea of using more of Hospice's services. We could request regular visits from the Hospice counselor, the music therapist and the chaplain.

When the three of us met with the Hospice counselor before Kris formally enrolled, he gave us information about what to expect with the progression of her illness. He explained Hospice's services and his availability to all of us throughout this final phase of her life. Because of their early connection with him, Kris and Sally were open to meeting with him during Kris's last eleven months. He was a great source of help and comfort to all of us.

When I was feeling close to burnout, I scheduled an individual session with him. Having the opportunity to pour out my feelings and be listened to in such a compassionate way gave me—one of the primary caregivers—renewed energy.

That period of time reminded me of the first year after my divorce. Twenty-five years ago I was balancing my responsibilities as a university professor with the responsibilities of being a single parent. One particularly stressful evening I came home to my apartment with no food in the refrigerator. My four-year-old daughter was crying, and she needed attention. I was totally depleted. I broke down crying, too.

Then I got myself into a more resourceful state, called a student and asked her if I could pay her to grocery shop for me. I had never heard of such a thing in 1981. I just knew I needed to reach out for help because I couldn't do it all myself. What I learned back then served me during this time with Kris.

I wondered how I would get Kris and Sally to accept more help. A breakthrough came when I reminded them how they had resisted getting a hospital bed. After it arrived and Kris spent nights in the new bed, they each rested more comfortably.

I suggested that they start having someone come in at night. This would provide many advantages. If someone else helped Kris during the night, Sally could sleep better and be more rested during the day. Another pair of eyes, ears and hands would be a big help during this time.

Finally, they gave in. Kris agreed, saying, "I can see it would help Sally."

Sally agreed, "Yes, let's do this for Kris."

With reluctance and trepidation they started accepting help in January. That was eight months after Kris's diagnosis and only three months before she died. They could have started using help about three months after the initial diagnosis.

While each remained strong in the belief that she didn't
need help, each accepted help for the other. I smiled and
thought to myself, "whatever works."

In the same manner, Kris decided hiring a personal chef
to stock the freezer was a good idea for Sally. Sally decided it
was a good idea because the personal chef could make meals
to Kris's taste.

When Sally finally requested help from Hospice, she had
a good time washing windows with the volunteer. This was a
task Sally and Kris had enjoyed doing together for many years.

Prior to Kris's illness, they had each encouraged the other
to get help with emotional issues. Counseling had been a
positive part of their lives for many years, both individually
and together. Having this structure in place before Kris got
sick made dealing with the emotional parts of the dying
process easier. For them, the challenges came when they
needed physical help and spiritual help. Those were the areas
that were new for them.

The first step to accepting help was recognizing the need
for help. This was difficult. I know I had an effect when I said,
"Everyone in your situation needs help. It's normal to need
help when you're going through this. Going through this life
transition is much like giving birth. It's generally accepted
today that when giving birth a woman needs help. I remember
giving birth to my daughter. It was so valuable to have help
from a number of people. My partner, the nurses, my
childbirth coach and others all helped me in significant ways.
Getting help from a number of people is normal and good.
These transitions are not that easy to navigate, and when
you've never done something before it's even harder. It makes

it so much better to have help. It's OK to ask for help. In fact, it's more than OK. Some might say it's your responsibility to ask for and accept help from lots of different people."

Both Kris and Sally were interested in the spiritual aspects of death. Neither one of them wanted to talk with someone who had a traditional religious philosophy. They declined the offer to talk with the Hospice chaplain, even though we were told the chaplain was non-denominational.

During the years before she got sick, Kris had read all of Neale Donald Walsch's books in the *Conversations With God* series. She also subscribed to his newsletter. The books present dialogues exploring philosophical questions about human existence, including discussions about love, faith, life, death, good and evil. Walsch's books assume the existence of a higher power. Although he uses the word "God," his approach is spiritual without being religious. These controversial books appeal to people from various traditions. I read them because they were important to Kris, and we had many discussions about ideas presented in the dialogues. During her illness, she received comfort from ideas she found in these books.

Kris felt a connection with her spiritual needs when she talked to me about her beliefs, hopes and fears. I listened to her with total acceptance.

Kris sought spiritual help when she asked me to meet with a psychic on her behalf. Through this process, Kris received validation that she had accomplished her life purpose and was complete. I understood the importance of Kris finding comfort during this final phase of life; I was happy to go to the psychic to help serve that purpose.

Kris asked for help finding someone to officiate at her memorial service. A friend recommended that we meet with the spiritual leader at Unity. Unity—www.unity.org—is a worldwide organization based on the spiritual principles of all the major world religions. This organization is an inclusive group that welcomes people of all faiths and provides support to spiritual seekers through prayer, publications and education. Kris, Sally and I met with the local Unity Spiritual Leader. We felt comfortable with her and liked her spiritual approach. She agreed to officiate at Kris's memorial service. After Kris died, Sally started attending Sunday morning services at Unity. She found her connection with that community comforting and uplifting.

Asking for and accepting help was an ongoing process. Learning to receive help was one of the "gifts" that Kris's illness provided to all of us.

14

UNFINISHED
BUSINESS

Given Kris's significant decision to reject chemotherapy and any measures that were offered to prolong her life, we talked earnestly about the things that she wanted to accomplish.

"Kris, what do you think about making a list of everything you want to do before you die?" I asked.

"I can do that," she said.

"I suggest you make it an open-ended list, adding and deleting things any time you wish," I continued.

"That sounds good," she said.

Even though I wanted to help make Kris's wishes come true, sometimes I was tempted to argue with her priorities. For example, when she learned her cancer had spread to her liver, she decided to buy new furniture and redecorate her home. I wanted to tell her all the reasons why it would be better to focus her limited time and energy on other things.

But, I reminded myself that this time was for Kris and her desires. It was important for her to exercise control over everything she could. The limited time that accompanied her approaching death made decisions seem of great consequence. I experienced the challenge of respecting her values and priorities when they were different from mine. By honoring and supporting her choices, I knew I was helping to improve the quality of this last phase of her life.

I talked with Kris's family about putting their needs aside until later. This was a time to let go of old disagreements and allow Kris the feeling of control. One way we could add to her peace of mind was to refrain from imposing our will on her. Our needs and wants could wait. Kris's could not.

I listened to her wishes and encouraged her while she bought new furniture and redecorated her home. She enjoyed being in control, and accomplishing that project gave her satisfaction.

During the eleven months following her diagnosis, Kris frequently added things to her list. For a while, whenever she completed items and crossed them off, she added others. It seemed she didn't want the list to get too short.

One day I noticed she added "complete scrapbook," but I didn't talk to her about it. After she died, Sally told me Kris had spent many hours completing her scrapbook. Apparently, that task was the process she used to review her life. Her purpose wasn't to leave the scrapbook to anyone in particular; she wished to provide herself with an overview and chronology of her life. Finishing the scrapbook was an important act of completion.

As her health declined and her physical energy waned, she took items off the list, saying they were no longer important. For example, she deleted "buy a new car." She also decided against visiting certain acquaintances. The list helped her focus attention each day on what was important to her.

She read the list each morning and chose one item to work on that day. Some days she worked on more than one thing. Some days she didn't feel well enough to work on anything.

While most of the things on Kris's list were ordinary activities, she also realized she needed to complete some emotional tasks. Shortly after learning that her illness was terminal, she talked about other types of unfinished business.

She said, "I need to resolve past hurtful incidents, both when I've been hurt and when I've hurt others. I know some people talk about forgiveness, but that's not the right word for me. I want to achieve resolution. You have already helped me resolve so much from my past. I know you can help me resolve other incidents so I can be at peace when I die. I know I can do that by writing letters and making amends. And I'd like your help."

I assured her that I would help her and that I had confidence she could resolve any unfinished business.

She told me, "In addition to everything else, there are two things that I need assurance about in regard to Sally.

- to be sure Sally can function independently
- to be sure Sally has my permission to move on with her life in the way that's best for her after I'm gone

"And there's one more thing—I've always worried about my little sister and her financial situation. I want to be sure she will be OK financially."

One of the things I admired about Kris was that she was a hard worker, constantly learning and improving herself. She wasn't about to stop now. I knew she was committed to doing her part to achieve the resolution that was so important.

Following are the tools and strategies we used to meet her desired outcomes.

Creating small tasks

We divided jobs into small, manageable tasks. I called that "chunking down." Kris had numerous books. Most of them were the "self-help" genre and related to how hard she worked to make herself a better person. When she looked at all her books she was overwhelmed and thought she'd never be able to sort them.

I told her there were two ways she could chunk down. She could look at one bookcase at a time, or if that was too much at once, she could look at one bookshelf at a time. Chunking down made the task of sorting the books manageable. A second way she could chunk down was by time. She could determine a reasonable amount of time to focus on her books. For example, she could set the timer for half an hour and sort her books until the timer rang.

She liked the idea of working on one bookcase at a time. She sorted her books into three categories—keep for Sally, give to friends, donate to the library. One day she had three big boxes of books for me. I put them into my lending library and often I sat with one of them and remembered her.

Passing on information

Kris wrote out instructions for Sally. She painstakingly wrote out in great detail how to program the sprinkler system. She also wrote down which kind of paint to use in each room and which service person to call when certain things went wrong in the house. Sally liked it that Kris wanted to do that for her. Sally was also reassured to have this information in writing. After Kris died, Sally liked reading things in Kris's handwriting.

Giving permission

Kris encouraged Sally to live life to the fullest after she was gone. She wanted Sally to actualize herself to the best of her ability, whatever that meant. She wanted to be sure the memory of their relationship didn't get in Sally's way of having the best possible life she could.

Even when Kris could no longer play golf, she made sure Sally did. Kris gave away her new golf clubs and bought golf clubs for other friends so they could play with Sally. Kris brought many people into their lives before she died so Sally would have those connections after her death.

Although Kris and Sally had no religious affiliation, Kris contacted the spiritual leader of Unity to perform her memorial service. Kris paved the way for Sally to become involved with a supportive spiritual group after she was gone.

Getting permission to die

Kris worried about Sally's ability to cope with life without her. Many times Sally reassured her, saying, "It's OK to go. I'll be OK on my own."

Furman and McNabb, authors of *The Dying Time*, stress the importance of telling a loved one who is dying three things.

- I love you
- It's OK to go
- I'll be all right without you

McNabb shares a tender, intimate moment when he sat down on the edge of his beloved's bed. Holding his hand and choked with emotion, he said, "My love, I want you to know that you have given meaning and purpose to my life. You have never been more loved than you are at this moment. I will be okay; I know that you can't help leaving me now. It has been the greatest honor to be loved by you. Know that I love you. I always will."

Furman and McNabb observe that almost all people who are dying can benefit from the permission of loved ones to make the transition in peace. They say, "Giving permission to your loved one does not hasten the death, it simply makes it emotionally easier."

Writing therapy letters

Kris wrote "therapy letters" to various people. These are letters that are written but that are never sent or given to anyone. They aren't censored or edited. Anything and everything is included in a therapy letter. It is OK to swear, say mean things and use any format. Spelling and grammar don't matter.

Kris wrote therapy letters to people who had hurt her in the past. She wrote them to neighbors from her childhood, a teacher and family members who were no longer alive. Some of the people she wrote letters to were nameless because she didn't remember their names.

These exercises were an opportunity for Kris to express her anger in a healthy way. She was able to discharge her anger instead of keeping it inside. As she worked on those letters she unearthed anger she didn't even remember she had. She marveled at how much she had kept hidden from her conscious mind.

Over and over again she expressed how spiritually and emotionally cleansed she felt by writing the therapy letters. Completing them made her feel more complete about her life. She said resolving so much from her past gave her internal peace.

Making amends

Before she died, Kris made amends for wrongs she had done in her lifetime. One day she spent a long time thinking and writing a letter to Sally. She specifically mentioned incidents where she had not behaved as she would have liked and that she wished she'd handled those situations differently. She offered a heartfelt apology for those times. She offered to make amends. It is a beautiful letter that Sally treasures.

Because Kris was unable to contact some of the people she had wronged, she made amends indirectly with financial donations to charitable causes. Instead of choosing a dollar amount for her amends, she chose a percentage of the money she had. She understood that she needed to make significant financial contributions for the amends to be meaningful.

Kris learned about restorative justice, a process where first-time offenders have the opportunity to right their wrongs. We talked about restorative justice versus punishment. This approach of making things right with someone resonated with her. She donated enough money to fund a local restorative justice training program for one year. Kris loved cars and was a firm believer in self-sufficiency. She donated money to a community program that provided used cars to women who were becoming self-sufficient. She designated her contribution for repair and maintenance of the cars.

Throughout the eleven months after her diagnosis, Kris spent much of her time and energy completing her unfinished business related to other people. Ira Byock, M.D., in *Dying Well*, gave an example of writing a "prescription" to help a dying patient complete relationships. This "prescription" was advice from the heart. He wrote what Hospice calls, "the five things of relationship completion."

- I forgive you
- Forgive me
- Thank you
- I love you
- Goodbye

By the time Kris died, she felt complete with her relationships. She also did exactly as she wished. She went to favorite restaurants, smoked whenever she wished, visited friends, shopped for clothes, read books about "the other side" and ate lots of desserts.

Completing all the things on her list gave her peace of mind. As she did these tasks she healed many old wounds, had some fun and gradually became ready to leave this life.

15

REMINISCING

I read somewhere that it is important to reminisce about sweet memories with a person who is dying. Much of what happens during the death and dying process is serious and stressful. Reminiscing about happy times provides relief from the physical and emotional intensity of the dying time. Everyone benefits from keeping in mind that many things in life are good, and some things are funny. It is pleasant to remember those times.

About six months into the process, Kris felt remarkably strong so I decided to ask her about the wonderful things she remembered.

"Kris, tell me about your favorite memories," I said.

With laughter in her eyes and a smile, she told me, "Sally and I have written some stories, which we want read at the memorial service. I want people who come to the service to know who I am."

Talking about those stories brought her obvious pleasure. She gave them to me to read. There were nine short narratives from different stages of her adulthood. She wrote about disregarding the law as a young adult—setting off a cherry bomb in college and later getting a speeding ticket in California. She shared stories of her developing construction and business skills in real estate projects—remodeling homes for profit and finding the run-down property that she turned into a dream home for Sally and her. And she wrote about enjoying her favorite things—her pets, shopping and being awake in the early morning hours.

These stories, although ordinary, painted a picture of Kris's life. In some respects, they served the same purpose as her scrapbook—a life review. She focused on stories that were enjoyable and amusing.

In discussing their decision to have the stories read at the memorial service, Sally quipped, "She sure wasn't going to have hymns and bible verses.

"We wanted to share stories about Kris so people could know her. We wanted people to enjoy the stories and if they were funny, all the better."

There were some stories that Kris wanted to include so she wrote those. Sally wrote the stories that were important to her. As they talked about the stories, they remembered more detail. Sometimes they remembered incidents in different ways, laughing and joking as they embellished the stories. They created precious memories as they reminisced.

Sally told Kris, "I really like my memory better than yours, so let's go with mine." Kris agreed as they bantered back and forth playfully.

They decided to exclude some stories because they didn't seem interesting or meaningful. When all the stories were written down, Sally edited them for structure and grammar.

Sometimes Kris and Sally cried as they recalled the stories, because they knew that soon there would be no more stories. "These are it," Kris said. The reality that she would die soon hung in the air even as they laughed about past events.

Sally told me, "It was an important, sharing time together that was fun. And working on that project was also sad because it was the end."

When Kris's sister came to visit, she and Kris spent time reminiscing about happy childhood memories. While that was fun and good, Kris also held many bad memories from her youth. She decided she only wanted stories from her adulthood shared at her memorial service because she had too much pain associated with her childhood. If she spent much time thinking about that part of her life, she got caught in a web of dark emotions.

Her sister wanted to include childhood stories to portray the special relationship between them. She treasured positive memories of being with Kris when they were children.

Any time there was a difference of opinion about what should be said or what should be done, we all agreed that Kris held the last word. We honored her wishes. Other people's feelings could be dealt with and worked through later. Kris's feelings could not. We worked hard to put her wishes first whenever possible.

There were two main reasons why it was so important to let Kris have her way.

- to allow her the feeling of control when there was so much in her life and her body that she couldn't control

- to help her create inner peace—an essential ingredient of dying well

If she had to fight for what she wanted, argue her point of view and give up control before it was necessary, she would be pulled away from her path of dying well.

"Writing the stories was harder for me than for Kris," Sally said. "She didn't seem sad. I didn't want the relationship to end. I didn't want Kris to go away. I was scared to death to be on my own."

Kris described the time they spent together writing stories as "bittersweet." During the last few months of her life, she used that word frequently.

Sally remembered, "Every time we were close or had fun, Kris called it bittersweet. We would revel in the good feelings, but we knew the end was near. We could never get away from that reality."

Reminiscing gave Kris an opportunity to think of herself and her life experiences in a positive light. Sally talked about Kris's identity, "For her, the biggest loss seemed to be the way she defined herself. She had always been powerful, independent, self-sufficient, competent, a person who acted with authority, in control. She knew what was best and had all the answers. She was a great orchestrator and could handle anything.

"When she learned her cancer was terminal, there was a gradual process of accepting the reality. As she got weaker and more disabled, she started seeing herself in a whole new light. She became quite demanding—not in a mean way. As her health declined, she needed more help. Being demanding was her way of being in control. She played that out in such a way that everyone responded just as she wished."

Sally summed it up by saying, "That's Kris—going out with a flair, with dignity."

That was the last of Kris's life stories.

16

GETTING AFFAIRS
IN ORDER & GIVING
AWAY PERSONAL
BELONGINGS

Long before Kris got sick, she and Sally had an attorney execute legal documents to protect their wishes regarding their relationship. Kris's Living Will stated that she didn't want any extraordinary means used to keep her alive. A Durable Power of Attorney gave Sally authority to make decisions regarding Kris's health care. Kris's Last Will and Testament provided for the distribution of her property and for cremation of her body after death.

About one month after Kris's diagnosis, she and Sally met with their attorney to review all the documents. Kris also made sure that her financial accounts either had Sally's name on them or had a "paid on death" provision. Kris made sure that all of her affairs were in order.

They went to their safety deposit box and brought Kris's Last Will and Testament and other important papers home. Safety deposit boxes are often sealed at death, so they brought everything Sally needed home.

Kris wanted to give away her possessions while she was still alive. In her relationship with Sally, Kris made most of the important decisions and worried that Sally wouldn't be able to cope without her. She knew that right after her death would be a challenging time of transition. She didn't want to burden Sally with the task of giving away numerous material possessions.

She made a list of all her belongings, indicating where she wanted them to go. Making a list to keep track of various items and where they were headed proved very helpful.

Early in the process she had to stop her exercise program because her illness drained her energy. So she made arrangements to send her treadmill, weights and related equipment to her sister's home in a neighboring state. She contacted a moving company to provide the transportation. When she lost interest in her computer, she also gave that to her sister who was happy to receive it.

Kris had a pocket knife that was meaningful to her. She wanted to give it to someone who would use it wisely. Although she didn't agree with the anti-gay stance of the Boy Scouts, she believed a boy scout would be someone who would appreciate her special knife and use it with positive intent.

Amazingly, I heard about a local boy scout who was struggling with cancer. She gave the knife to him with an explanatory note and then she purchased a set of Boy Scout knives to give to his entire troop. Giving the knives was an act of completion for her. I made sure the knives got to the troop leader because Kris had no interest in presenting the knives in person.

Even though Kris dressed casually and comfortably, her clothes showed her attention to detail and her appreciation of quality. She bought new clothes each season. During the winter when she realized it was the last year of her life, she boxed up her summer clothes and sent them to a group of women she knew would be grateful to have them.

As her ankles became swollen and she could no longer wear her socks, Kris offered them to me. Although this was an unusual gift, I graciously accepted her bag of fine socks, which were practically new. After she died, I felt comforted when I wore them.

As Kris gave away her belongings, she seemed to be loosening her ties to her life here. She also enjoyed the reactions of others who received her gifts.

Kris and Sally owned some rental houses as real estate investments. Kris always had the major responsibility for those properties. She listed them for sale and made sure they sold before she died. It gave her satisfaction to complete those projects and spare Sally the work that went with them.

Sally appreciated those actions. The emotional advantages of selling the properties before Kris died was a higher priority for both of them than any financial gain that would have occurred by waiting until after she died.

Kris was very attached to her vehicles. She was reluctant to stop driving, and it was hard for her to give up her latest, beloved SUV. Finally, she acknowledged she had to stop driving. As her illness progressed, she could no longer drive safely. Kris and Sally completed the paperwork necessary to change legal ownership of the vehicle to Sally. Kris liked thinking that after her death Sally would be driving her SUV. Sally liked driving the vehicle that was so important to Kris.

There were many times we talked about distributing her money. Our dialogues went something like this:

Kris: I think it's important to give away my money now. But what if I live another year?

Me: It's important that you do exactly what feels right to you.

Kris: I would like to give away my money, but I might need it.

Me: You can keep it now and know that it will go to your beneficiaries after you're gone.

Kris: It will be better if I give it away while I'm still here, keeping only what I need.

Me: You can do that and know if it turns out that you're here longer than planned, Sally will pay for whatever you need.

Kris: I don't want to be dependent on Sally or anyone else.

Me: That's fine. You can keep a cushion so you feel comfortable with that.

Kris: I think it's important to give away my money now. But what if I live another year?

We went round and round on this topic. The conversation was an example of getting stuck in a particular way of thinking based on fears. Kris was struggling with inner conflict between her desire to give her money away and her fear that she wouldn't have enough. Talking aloud about difficult topics helped her sort out her thoughts and feelings. Getting input from a trusted, outside source was invaluable in helping her think and also in feeling supported in whatever decision she made.

As Kris's health declined and she had more limitations, it became easier for her to give money away. She knew that at the time of her death the money in her accounts would be paid to Sally. Kris had a strong need to know her younger sister would be financially secure. Before Kris died, she paid off her sister's debts, which contributed to peace of mind for both of them. Kris sent a check to her mother and a check to her older sister. These actions helped her feel complete about money and her family of origin.

During Kris's last eleven months of life, Sally supported Kris's choices for the disposition of her money and her personal belongings. That was good for Kris because these topics had the potential for being a source of conflict between her and Sally.

When Kris wanted to give something away, no one argued with her. I was glad no one tried to convince her to keep something because of some monetary or sentimental value. Kris always exercised strict control over her affairs. As her illness progressed, she lost control of so much. Distributing her money and her belongings were areas where we could support her decisions and allow her control.

After Kris's death, Sally was grateful she only had a few of Kris's things left. It would have been a physical and emotional burden for Sally to sort through Kris's belongings and decide what to do with them.

Kris was right. Distributing her things while she was still alive was best for both her and Sally.

17

PHYSICAL AIDS & PROFESSIONAL SERVICES

After Kris's diagnosis and her decision to reject treatment, she was able to function in her usual way for a few months. As her illness progressed, she and Sally found they needed many physical aids. Hospice provided most of them. Kris and Sally found others at a specialty drugstore near the hospital, on the Internet and through catalogues.

Although Hospice provided a basic version of all the mobility aids, Kris often preferred to buy her own at a specialty medical supply business. At her request, her equipment was donated to the local AIDS project after her death.

In addition to physical aids, Kris and Sally found personal professional services that eased the process.

Kris said, "If only there were a list of these things somewhere."

I agreed. A list of goods and services for the dying would have been helpful. As I talked with others who had gone through this difficult process, many people expressed frustration at not knowing what products and services would help them. Often when they learned about products and services, they didn't know where to find them. The Internet can be overwhelming because of the quantity of available merchandise. Plus, judging the quality of items and vendors is difficult.

For the most part, I have avoided endorsing specific vendors except for the Vermont Country Store. It is a family-owned business that has been operating since 1946. It is known for its quality merchandise (for example, Lanz of Switzerland sleepwear, Lotil cream, Vinola soap) and outstanding customer service. The store carries many items that are difficult to find elsewhere—www.vermontcountrystore.com.

Although each death is different and patients' needs vary, we eventually found numerous things to help make Kris comfortable. Following is a list of services and items that helped Kris complete her life the way she wanted. In order to reduce stress and prevent crises, I suggest that you start looking for products and arranging for services early in the process. These are guidelines that most people will find helpful during the dying time.

Professional Services

Psychotherapist or coach

Having one person committed to guide the death and dying process was invaluable. I kept noticing the similarities between dying and birthing. Just as women are assisted by birthing teachers, I thought about how much was gained by having a therapist or coach to help with dying.

A coach helps people learn about the options available at the end of life, helps them decide how they want to die and then helps to guide the experience. Coaches enhance the quality of people's lives, and end-of-life is no exception. The International Coach Federation—www.coachfederation.org—defines coaching in the following manner:

"Professional coaches provide an ongoing partnership designed to help clients produce fulfilling results in their personal and professional lives. Coaches help people improve their performances and enhance the quality of their lives.

"Coaches are trained to listen, to observe and to customize their approach to individual client needs. They seek to elicit solutions and strategies from the client; they believe the client is naturally creative and resourceful. The coach's job is to provide support to enhance the skills, resources, and creativity that the client already has."

Hospice

Following is an excerpt from www.caringinfo.org:

"What is hospice?

"Considered to be the model for quality, compassionate care for people facing a life-limiting illness or injury, hospice and palliative care involve a team-oriented approach to expert medical care, pain management, and emotional and spiritual support expressly tailored to the patient's needs and wishes. Support is provided to the patient's loved ones as well.

"The focus of hospice relies on the belief that each of us has the right to die pain free and with dignity, and that our loved ones will receive the necessary support to allow us to do so.

"Hospice focuses on caring, not curing and in most cases care is provided in the patient's home.

- Hospice care also is provided in freestanding hospice centers, hospitals, and nursing homes and other long-term care facilities.
- Hospice services are available to patients of any age, religion, race, or illness.
- Hospice care is covered under Medicare, Medicaid, most private insurance plans, HMOs, and other managed care organizations."

For more information on Hospice, visit www.hospice.com and conduct an Internet search.

Non-medical caregivers

At my request, Hospice gave us a list of local businesses that provided in-home care. We interviewed these businesses before the need became urgent. Many communities have businesses that provide whatever help you need, including grocery shopping, picking up prescriptions, making phone calls, helping with pet care and doing errands.

Kris and Sally needed prodding to hire someone to provide all-night care. When they finally agreed, they were happily surprised that both of them slept better.

When the caregiver was at their home, she did some light housework and provided care for Kris when she needed it. The caregiver often helped with laundry and grocery shopping.

Personal chef

Sally hired a personal chef to prepare a month's worth of dinners. Having these available in the freezer ensured that Sally got the nutrition she needed even when she was feeling overwhelmed.

House cleaning service

Hiring someone to clean the house made everything easier. It not only lightened Sally's work load, it made the environment seem lighter and brighter.

Sleeping

Hospital bed

Even though Kris and Sally initially resisted bringing a hospital bed into their home, both of them were glad when it arrived. Kris liked the bed immediately. She found it more comfortable than her regular bed because of all the adjustment possibilities. Both of them slept better with Kris in the hospital bed. Placing the bed in the living room in front of the picture window allowed Kris to feel included in the household activity and to enjoy the view when she was alone.

Alternating pressure air mattress

Placing this air mattress on top of the hospital bed made a big difference to Kris. This product was available from the health care company that provided oxygen and durable medical equipment. The business delivered the air mattress already inflated so it was easy to make adjustments by inflating or deflating it. I was surprised when Kris discovered that letting some air out of it made it more comfortable.

Disposable mattress protectors

Keeping a disposable pad on top of the sheets was an easy way to protect the bedding from involuntary bodily discharge.

Blanket

As Kris's illness progressed, her skin became more and more sensitive. Finding covers that kept her warm and were comfortable on her body was a challenge. She was happy with a very lightweight down blanket that she ordered from The Vermont Country Store catalogue.

Bedside table on wheels

This table swings over the bed and provides much-needed space and support. This is the same type of table commonly used in hospitals.

Baby monitor

This two-piece device is designed to allow parents to hear their baby while in different places in the house. One part of the baby monitor was by Kris's hospital bed and the other part was in the family room with the night-time caregiver. The baby monitor made it possible for the caregiver to respond while still allowing Kris her privacy.

Mobility

Cane

There are numerous canes to choose from on the Internet. We found that a wooden one was best because it could be cut to the exact height that was right for Kris. She also liked how it looked. That was important because she was self-conscious about her appearance.

Walker

We found it very handy to have a walker equipped with a basket on it to carry her portable oxygen tank. Having a walker with four wheels and hand brakes became more important as her illness progressed and she became weaker.

Wheelchair

We learned that wheelchairs are sized to the person. A chair that is properly sized is comfortable and provides good support.

Lift

There are manual and hydraulic lifts available from medical supply companies. These devices are beneficial to patients and their caregivers.

Personal Hygiene

Padded toilet seats

As her mobility became impaired, Kris requested raised toilet seats. Because she was barely five foot three inches tall, the standard raised toilet seats were too high. She switched to padded toilet seats which provided a little more height than regular seats. She said they were just right for her.

Bedside commode

When Kris could no longer get to the bathroom, the Hospice nurse provided a commode. She placed it conveniently next to Kris's hospital bed.

Wet wipes

Kris appreciated having wet wipes in every bathroom. Once she needed the bedside commode, we moved the wet wipes there to help with toilet hygiene.

Hand-held shower head

Kris and Sally had a plumber install a hand-held shower head, which made bathing easier than using a fixed shower head.

Shower stool

This stool provided by Hospice allowed Kris to sit in the shower while Sally helped bathe her.

Extra soft washcloth and towel

As Kris's illness progressed, she wanted a new washcloth and towel that were extraordinarily soft. We never found quite the right solution to this problem.

Dry shampoo with conditioner in a shower cap

This product made it possible to wash Kris's hair without water while she was still in bed. It looked like a shower cap and once in place Sally could rub it all over Kris's head. Then the cap was removed and Kris's hair could be brushed. Her hair looked clean, and she said it felt good, too. The nurses used this product on Kris's hair when she was in the hospital for her emergency surgery. I was able to find a similar product with an Internet search for "dry shampoo."

Special lotions

Kris found special lotions in The Vermont Country Store catalogue that helped her feel more comfortable. She used Lotil on her hands and found it especially helpful for cuts around her fingernails. She used a face cream called Retinol, a vitamin A enriched day cream with SPF 20 sunscreen. Lubriderm was recommended by a dermatologist as a good body lotion. Kris said the lotion helped keep her skin comfortable.

Skin condition varies quite a lot from person to person. How much skin deteriorates during the dying process depends on many variables, including where a person lives, the illness, age, skin condition prior to the illness and the length of the dying time.

Soap

The Vermont Country Store catalogue sells a soap called Vinola that has a wonderful scent and works as a great moisturizer.

Salve

Kris put Boroleum in her nostrils to keep them moist. Unfortunately, she couldn't use this salve very long because we learned it is flammable and can't be used around supplemental oxygen. After Kris died, I learned there are non-petroleum based products that can be used with oxygen. I found them on the Internet by searching for "non-petroleum based salve."

Clothes

Loose and soft night clothes

Kris and Sally worked hard to find clothes that were loose, soft and comfortable on Kris's skin. I learned from the Hospice nurse that some people in the end stage of their lives are more comfortable sleeping naked.

Socks with extra wide tops

These socks are advertised for people with diabetes. Most people in the terminal stage of an illness retain water, causing their legs to swell. Tight socks are uncomfortable.

Maternity pants

People who choose not to take traditional cancer treatments discover a troubling side effect—abdominal tumors continue to grow and can become quite large. Obviously, this adds to physical discomfort.

Maternity pants allow room as tumors grow. These pants also come in a variety of styles. In Kris's case, she could continue to dress in blue jeans—her favorite.

Medicine

Pillboxes

As Kris's health declined, her medicine regimen became more and more complicated. Having a system that grouped pills according to day and time of day was essential.

Oxygen

Kris had two in-home, large-capacity oxygen tanks that were placed in the closet of a spare bedroom. She also had portable oxygen tanks that lasted three to four hours each. A humidifier could be attached to an oxygen tank to prevent the nostrils from getting uncomfortably dry. At the end of Kris's life, we turned up the oxygen to the highest setting to make it easier for her to breathe. After she died, we learned that the extra oxygen may have prolonged her life. Caregivers need to be aware that there are pros and cons to increasing the oxygen. According to authors Furman and McNabb, "Whereas oxygen generally decreases the struggle to breathe toward the end of life, high flow rates of oxygen may prolong the dying process."

Pain medicine

We called Hospice when Kris was in pain. A Hospice nurse was always available to consult, and the help proved invaluable. Kris took her pain medicine in a combination of regularly scheduled pills and supplemental liquid as needed. The pain medicine made Kris more comfortable and also induced drowsiness. The nurse explained to us that some people like more, and some people like less pain medicine. The choice is a balance between comfort and alertness.

There are considerations to increasing morphine for pain control. In *The Dying Time*, Furman and McNabb tell us, "While morphine decreases anxiety and depresses the physiological urge to breathe, at high doses toward the end of life it may shorten the dying process."

We were very grateful to our Hospice nurse who made sure Kris felt very little pain—even during her last few days when she could no longer swallow pills. Pain medicines are also administered by injection, with a continuous drip or through patches worn on the skin.

Food and Drink

Glass with a top and a flexible straw

Kris always wanted water by her bed. She used a plastic twelve-ounce tumbler with a few ice cubes in it. Having a top on the glass prevented spills when it was accidentally knocked over.

Meal replacement bars and drinks

Many companies make meal-replacement bars and drinks that are available at the grocery store. They were handy when Kris felt hungry but didn't find any food appealing. Because she had hypoglycemia, she felt better when she ate foods sweetened with fructose or sugar substitutes. We found bars and shakes that were developed for diabetics met her nutritional needs.

Sugar-free ice cream

In the last few weeks, Kris ate ice cream with nuts—almonds, pecans, walnuts—everyday because that's what appealed to her. The ice cream and nuts added joy to her life. Kris ate small quantities of regular food and ice cream until she quit eating, two days before she died.

Miscellaneous

Rice pack

This healing product—which is similar to a bean bag—comes in various sizes and shapes. Rice packs are usually made with soft cloth. They can be warmed in the microwave oven and placed on any part of the body. Placing it on Kris's legs and feet provided comforting warmth and helped make leg and foot cramps go away.

Rice packs are available in health food stores, on the Internet and in specialty shops. They can also be made with soft flannel using measurements of the specific user. For example, a wing-shaped rice pack could be made to fit around the neck and shoulder.

3M picture hooks

At the end of her life, Kris spent most of her time in her hospital bed facing the picture window in the living room. She had her oxygen tanks placed in a closet in a nearby bedroom. The plastic tubing was run from the bedroom to the living room along the juncture of the wall and the ceiling, held in place by 3M picture hooks. This kept the tubing out of the way without marring the walls. Without the picture hooks the cats would have destroyed the plastic tubing.

Nicotine patches or nicotine gum

Since Kris was adamant about smoking outside, switching to another form of nicotine would have made things easier for her and her caregivers. Medical providers frequently recommend using these alternatives as an aid to quitting smoking. The Hospice nurse told us she could put a nicotine patch on Kris at the end of her life if she started having withdrawal symptoms when she was no longer physically able to smoke.

Whenever we suggested that Kris try the nicotine patches or nicotine gum, she said she wasn't ready yet. Because we knew it was important to support her wishes, her caregivers expended great effort to get her out of bed and outside the house to smoke until she no longer asked for cigarettes. She never used the patches or the gum. She smoked her last cigarette two days before she died.

Small table fan

Kris enjoyed having a small fan near her bed. Even though the house was kept at a temperature of 72 degrees for her, she liked the movement of the air. The Hospice nurse recommended a fan blowing on Kris because people with COPD (Chronic Obstructive Pulmonary Disease) usually find the breeze comforting.

Sally and I talked about all the different ways we worked at making Kris comfortable and happy during her illness.

As Sally said, "Kris was the lucky recipient. In dying, she was the center of the world. The world revolved around her."

Once again, the dying time reminded me of life with a new baby. Kris's beautiful spirit took center stage and many people provided all that was needed. So much was needed. It was both exhausting and enriching to be part of the process.

Fortunately, many resources are available—although it took some work to find them.

18

PLANNING
THE SERVICE

A few months after the diagnosis, Kris and Sally grew into a reluctant acceptance of their situation. I encouraged them to start planning the type of memorial service they wanted for Kris. While neither was religious, they both felt that a service was important and necessary.

We didn't know how long Kris would live, and we were mindful that cancer could affect her brain as her illness progressed. I knew that for Kris to be involved in the decisions and planning, we had to start early.

"Kris, what kind of service do you want?" I asked.

She responded by saying, "I think we should visit some funeral homes before we choose one."

"Yes," I said, "and you don't have to use a funeral home if you don't want. You can do this however you want in the way that's best for you."

She thought for a few minutes and then said, "I think it'll be easiest if we use a funeral home."

We decided to interview three local funeral homes to see their facilities and to talk about how services were conducted. Kris was still walking without physical aids when we visited them. This was eight months before Kris died.

We went to three funeral homes in a period of two months. We planned a few questions ahead of time. Because we were ignorant about the process of arranging a funeral or a memorial service, we weren't sure what questions to ask. We listened a lot and toured the buildings. Each of the funeral homes had a different look and feel to it. We learned it was unusual for people to visit ahead of time. Our visits were invaluable in helping Kris and Sally decide which funeral home they wanted to use.

When Kris and Sally started talking about the service, they quickly decided to focus on honoring Kris's life rather than mourning her death. Kris knew she wanted to be cremated, and Sally was comfortable with that decision. It was Kris's wish to be cremated with two beloved stuffed bears and her special blanket.

We learned that with cremation, if any family member objects, you must have a paragraph in your will naming a "personal representative for cremation" who will faithfully represent your wishes. For Kris and Sally, cremation posed no problems. But, this issue is sometimes a source of conflict for families.

After Kris died, I found out that some crematoriums allow mourners to be present at the cremation, and anyone can make that request of the funeral director. Sally and I weren't interested in that option.

In visiting funeral homes we learned new vocabulary.

- **Pre-need**—before death
- **At need**—at death
- **Visitation**—having people view the body
- **Folder**—the folded piece of paper, or booklet, that serves as a program for the service
- **Cremains**—slang for the ashes that result from the cremation
- **Cremated remains**—the proper term for "cremains"

We discovered quickly that funeral home directors are very focused on talking about money. That's what each of them talked about first. When we objected, they explained this was because of legal regulations. We learned to let them know that we wanted our time with them to be about planning the memorial service, and we preferred to have written information about the fees to look at later.

Once we got that discussion out of the way, the funeral homes gave us some helpful checklists. Examples included:

- Make a list of everyone who helps and how they helped
- Send thank you notes to people who bring food, send flowers or send contributions
- Put name labels on plates or food containers so you know where to return them
- Get a guest book for the service to help you remember who attended

Our first funeral home visit was not a positive experience. The funeral director was called away on an emergency, and we met with a substitute. We were very uncomfortable with him. His dark suit, business-like mannerisms and formality made us uncomfortable. We didn't feel we belonged there. The whole process was unfamiliar, intimidating and cold.

Even some of the décor of the funeral home seemed strange. Although by the end of our visit, I appreciated the creative way the funeral home provided tissues. The first thing I saw in the lobby was a large pottery vase filled with little packets of Kleenex instead of flowers. I picked up a packet of Kleenex and put it in my purse. Later, when I felt teary, the tissues came in handy.

Leaving the funeral home, we made some jokes to lighten things up. Kris and Sally repeated that they wanted the memorial service to be a celebration of Kris's life, not a solemn, formal affair.

Our visit to the second funeral home wasn't any better. On the positive side, we were more familiar with the process. We knew more questions to ask and had a basis for comparison. On the negative side, the building was older and darker, and the atmosphere was depressing. There were numerous crosses and other religious artifacts throughout the building. We didn't stay very long. After seeing the second funeral home, the first one didn't seem so bad.

The first funeral home we went to was new with lots of windows. The building had a bright and airy feel to it. The setting was comfortable and conducive to talking with the staff about what we wanted and didn't want.

"Kris," I said, "How would it be if I called the first funeral home again and made an appointment to meet with someone else?" Kris and Sally thought that was a good idea. Meanwhile, we visited the third funeral home. When we arrived there for our appointment, we met a funeral director who was dressed formally and had just stepped out of a hearse. The initial conversation with him was about hearses, the flow of traffic at funerals and parking problems. I felt as if we were in a weird movie.

When I called to make an appointment to return to the first funeral home, I explained what went wrong with our previous meeting and what would make it comfortable for us to return. Among other things, I mentioned Kris wasn't a coffee drinker; she liked iced tea. They were accommodating.

When we arrived for our appointment, three funeral directors met us. In addition to the male senior director, there was a female funeral director and a delightful, easy-going young man in training. The administrative assistant also came to our meeting. She was warm and friendly and shared helpful stories.

The greeting and the warmer demeanor of the group put us at ease. As a result of my specific feedback and requests, they all greeted us by name, shook our hands, made eye contact and served us iced tea. We felt welcomed and more comfortable than the first time. We explained more clearly what we wanted and what we needed. They listened more and we talked more. We agreed this was the best funeral home for our purpose.

Because we started planning the service eight months before Kris died, Kris had time to choose photos, poems and music for the service. Kris and Sally made a list of people to invite. They scheduled the event at 10 a.m. on a Saturday to make it convenient for people to attend. A reception would follow with Kris's favorite music playing in the background. Once we knew the date of the service, Sally and I called everyone on the list to invite them.

When we met with the spiritual leader of Unity, she gave us an outline of a memorial service that focused on celebrating Kris's life. Kris, Sally and I were invited to make any changes we wanted.

I remember thinking this was just like a wedding ceremony. We could use a "canned formula" that would be acceptable, although boring and sterile. Or, we could plan our own beautiful and meaningful ceremony. The latter required time and energy; it was well worth the effort.

In preparing for the memorial service, the spiritual leader asked both Sally and me to write a list of adjectives describing Kris. Our lists were primarily made up of positive attributes. Because all three of us wanted to be authentic, we also included some words that were less flattering.

I wrote:
- Life partner, sister, daughter, aunt, friend;
- Committed to self-improvement, smart, good learner, voracious reader, articulate, able to admit mistakes, responsible for her actions—good and bad;
- Competent, hard-working, self-reliant, assertive, responsible, conscientious;
- Respectful of others, always on time, meticulous, orderly, sometimes perfectionist, always well-groomed;
- Persistent, honest, trustworthy, courageous, brave, strong;

- Intuitive, good listener, kind, caring, considerate, generous, philanthropic;
- Adventurous, loving toward animals;
- Multi-faceted, able to connect with people from all walks of life and different social classes;
- Tenacious, deep thinker, champion of the underdog, opinionated, sometimes bossy.

Sally wrote:
- Best friend, giver, soft, fun to be with, gentle, loving, playful, silly, funny;
- Beautiful listener, speaks with honesty and clarity;
- Imaginative, creative, compassionate, empathic;
- Intelligent, thinker, intuitive, perceptive, keenly tuned into human nature and human behavior;
- Worked very hard all her life, holds self to high standards, so much integrity;
- Planner, organizer, steward of the earth;
- Interior decorator, exterior designer;
- Entertaining, good cook, made the best pumpkin pie;
- Quick temper, controlling.

Sally and I shared our lists with Kris. We took turns reading them to her aloud. They made her smile with an expression that said, "You really know me very well."

These lists were read at the service, giving people a chance to reflect on Kris's character and personality. All of us were encouraged to think about how each word might apply to us and how we could learn something about ourselves from Kris's life.

When we were at the funeral home, we looked at sample folders. Later, Kris created a rough draft of what she wanted. Her folder was a simple 5½" by 8½" piece of paper folded in half. It had four pages. The front had a photograph of Kris with her date of birth and date of death. The inside left page provided a list that described how she wanted to be remembered. The inside right page was the program for the service, listing poems read and songs sung. The back page was a favorite poem about death.

Over the next few months I worked closely with Ellen, the administrative assistant, to prepare the folder. She worked with us through many revisions to prepare the folder just the way we wanted. We chose the card stock, the size, the font, and had it all laid out except for the date of death. Ellen was very accepting of my perfectionist tendencies. It was great to have her as a contact so we could call and ask questions as they arose. After Kris died, Ellen inserted the date of death and ran off fifty folders—the approximate number of people we expected to attend the service.

We had difficulty predicting how many people would come to the service, and Sally worried that not many people would show up. The funeral home was flexible with two different rooms we could use. They said if fewer than fifty people came we would go to the smaller room; if more showed up, we'd use the larger room.

Sally believed the number of people who came to the service was an indication of the importance of Kris's life. We talked about why that was not a useful or accurate interpretation.

She said, "What if only five or ten people show up?"

"Sally" I said, "How many people's lives do you think were affected by Kris during her lifetime?"

She smiled and felt better when she shifted her focus to remember that Kris touched many people while she was alive. She realized that what occurred while Kris was alive was most important—not the number of people who attended her memorial service.

After we talked about it, Sally knew that the number of people who came to the service would be exactly right. If only five or ten people showed up, that would be perfect and would allow special things to happen that could only happen in a group that size. The number of people who came to the service didn't mean anything about the importance of Kris's life.

About fifty people came to the service. That made it possible to meet in the smaller room with an intimate feel. Kris wasn't a formal person, and the size of the room helped create an informal atmosphere which represented how Kris lived her life. At her service, there was time and space for everyone who wanted to speak.

The service was warm and meaningful. The early preparation helped put people at ease. Even though Kris wouldn't be there, she had imagined the event and was with us in spirit. Kris's memorial service was a special occasion filled with love.

19

HOW MUCH
TIME DO I
HAVE LEFT?

Often Kris asked, "How much time do I have left?"
She asked her oncologist, she asked her Hospice
nurse, she asked her Hospice counselor and she asked a
psychic. She found none of the answers satisfactory. No
one would—or could—tell her an estimated time of death.
Frustrated by what she felt was a lack of information, she
urged me to talk with people privately to see if I could get
a better response.

When we first met with our local Hospice program in
July, a nurse wouldn't give a time estimate but explained to
us what to look for as the illness progressed. "Expect more
fatigue, appetite decrease, discomfort on the right side,
indigestion, being full after two bites of food, swelling in the
ankles, trouble moving bowels, food not tasting right, food
not going down right."

With much prodding, while I spoke to the nurse privately, she finally said, "I'd be surprised if Kris is here a year from now."

Six weeks before Kris died, the Hospice counselor told me, "Her timeline looks short. It looks like a couple of weeks, but because of the strength of her willpower I expect it to be longer."

He explained that Kris was showing mixed messages, "She has the pain and agitation characteristic of the last week or two, and she's still showing interest in the big wide world. It's unusual for someone with only one or two weeks left to go to restaurants and follow current events."

The tendency for terminally ill patients to want to know how much time they have left is natural, so it wasn't surprising that Kris kept asking this question. She was particularly tenacious in her pursuit of a timeline. She knew that the quality of each day was more important than attempting to determine a date. Still, she wanted to know.

When she tired of asking the medical professionals, she turned to the more ethereal realm. She asked me to pose the question to a psychic. The psychic didn't provide a specific prediction. The words she channeled from Kris's spirit guides were, "Kris is meant to be leaving here before long. We can't tell the amount of time. That is between her and Spirit. It will be when it is right for her."

Those words provided a comforting explanation. We felt reassured that Kris's dying process would happen exactly as it was supposed to happen.

Still, the medical providers explained some details that although strange and unfamiliar, were very useful. A nurse told us about two different breathing patterns common in patients close to death. She said both may be disconcerting for loved ones but are not a problem for the patient and don't require intervention.

- **Cheyne-Stokes (pronounced chain-stokes) respiration.** Loved ones may hear a struggle while the patient takes a breath. This is followed by a brief period of ten to thirty seconds with no breathing. This pattern can go on for hours. Kris never exhibited Cheyne-Stokes respiration.
- **The death rattle.** Sometimes when a person is close to death, mucus accumulates in the back of the throat, causing a characteristic rattle sound during breathing. When we heard Kris make this sound, we knew it was a normal part of the process.

At the beginning of April, in response to our incessant questions about how much longer Kris would live, a nurse told us that one of three things was likely to cause Kris's death. She presented the following possibilities:

- Pneumonia or some other infection—at Kris's request, no antibiotics would be administered. An infection would cause a high fever and hasten death.
- Liver failure—she would become jaundiced, her skin would turn yellow/orange, and she would die.
- Lack of oxygen—Kris retained a lot of fluid in her abdomen. The fluid would eventually move to her lungs, and she would become increasingly short of breath and die.

I also knew from reading Sherwin Nuland, M.D.'s, *How We Die* that the disease could cause a general shutting down of the organs and body functions. As our Hospice nurse said, "When there's a general shutting down, it's the body's way of knowing it won't get better, and it's time to stop functioning."

Early in the process, I was prepared for Kris's death. I went to a convention in November, three months into the illness and planned to return early if she died. As the months continued, Sally and I became more and more physically and emotionally drained. Attending to Kris became a way of life, and it seemed there was no end in sight. Kris's needs were overwhelming. Often during those months, I was reminded of the exhaustion I felt years ago adapting to life with a new baby.

As the months passed, I sometimes felt deep sadness. Other times I felt anger. Sometimes, I wasn't aware of any feelings. I had no time to deal with my feelings or much of anything else in my life.

With each decline I adjusted, although at times I thought I couldn't go on. The only way I kept going was to keep my focus on the present moment. I didn't let myself think about how long it had been since we learned Kris was dying. And I didn't let myself think about how much longer it would be until she died. By the end, we were all worn out.

At the beginning of the week that Kris died, she declined noticeably. The Hospice nurse told us that Kris could stay alive in this condition for weeks. By then, we were all running on empty and somewhat numb. Eleven months of this seemed like a very long time. We did everything we could to keep going, knowing we would go on as long as Kris was alive.

After a while, I almost forgot that Kris would die because I was so focused on dealing with each moment of her life. That made the actual moment of death more difficult for me. It snuck up on me. It never occurred to me that Kris would die that night. I was gearing up for another long week.

In spite of all the planning, I was totally surprised— caught off guard, blindsided—when Kris died. At this stage of exhaustion, euphemisms such as, "Her timeline is short" and "She'll be leaving soon" didn't register.

Perhaps no one was direct because to say that Kris would die soon would be to state the obvious. In retrospect, it seems hard to believe I was surprised. As I look back now, I know that I saw all the signs that everyone else saw. Yet, being so close and so exhausted, I was unable to see that her death was imminent.

Only after Kris died, did we learn the answer to her question—eleven months.

20

A FINAL
LETTING GO

As Kris's illness progressed, she kept her focus on what was important to her during the time she had left to live. During her last eleven months, she never talked with me about her frustration or anger. I realize now it may have been useful to ask Kris about those feelings.

Schedules and routine had always been important to her, and that continued to be true during her illness. Before she got sick, eating meals out structured Kris's life, and she talked about how precious that time was for her and Sally to have deep, meaningful conversations. At the end of her life, going out to restaurants became her reason to live.

Because going out to breakfast was paramount to Kris, Sally did all she could to keep their routine. When Kris's sister visited for the last time, she saw the extraordinary efforts and struggle needed to get Kris to their vehicle.

"Kris, you can't do this anymore. Someone's going to get hurt if you keep it up," her sister said.

Then Sally described the time she and Kris fell down in the garage. Each day it got harder to move Kris from the hospital bed into the car even though it was only a few steps to the garage. It was no easy task to get her in and out of the wheelchair. Transferring her from the chair to the vehicle took an enormous amount of strength. And it was just as difficult to get her back in the wheelchair when they returned home.

One day, as Sally was doing her best to get Kris from the vehicle into the house, both of them fell on the floor in the garage. Kris hit her head on the concrete floor, but neither of them was seriously hurt.

Sally told me about all the times at the restaurant Kris closed her eyes and appeared to be sleeping. When Kris had to go to the bathroom, it was a major ordeal. These restaurant outings went on long after they were pleasurable for Sally and long after they were safe for the couple. The trips were almost impossible for Sally to manage by herself, although she never complained nor did she ever tell anyone how hard it was for her until after Kris died.

When Kris's sister came to visit, it was the first time that anyone became aware of the situation. Her sister saw that it was dangerous to continue these trips, and she confronted Kris.

Kris was adamant about continuing to go out to breakfast. She argued, but in her weakened condition she was no match for her sister. She lost the argument and initially was angry about her loss.

Then, she relented and seemed to accept the change. Once she and Sally stopped those outings Kris relaxed and stopped pushing herself. She stopped interacting with the world and stopped eating. She died peacefully a few days later.

There were only two times that Kris expressed anger during her last eleven months. Both times involved her sister. The first was when her sister put a stop to going out to breakfast, and Kris put up a fight. The second was when her sister went shopping for new pajamas for Kris. Kris didn't like them and lashed out at her.

Kris cared deeply about her younger sister and wanted to take care of her. Sometimes, she worried that her sister would have trouble managing her life without Kris's help. I wondered if Kris needed to be angry at her to make it easier to let go. After her sister left, Kris told me they had completed their relationship. I knew this final letting go was necessary for Kris to have a peaceful death.

21

THE DAY
KRIS DIED

K ris and I talked often about the moment of death.
She expressed her fear of getting lost and going in the
wrong direction after she left her body.

I said, "Tell me how you want it to be. Describe your
optimal scenario."

When she wasn't sure how to answer, I offered
suggestions and asked questions. "As you make the transition
from this world to the next, I've read that some people think
there's an angel that greets you and helps you go in the right
direction. Would that be helpful to you?"

"Yes," she said, and I saw her body relax.

I suggested to Kris that her only task at the moment of
death would be to follow the light. Many people who have
had near-death experiences describe a wonderful and
comforting light that they moved toward. Whenever Kris
expressed fear about the transition, I said to her softly, "just
follow the light." That always helped her to relax.

One day during a friend's visit, Kris explained that she feared not being able to make the transition safely. This friend, who had psychic skills, said, "At the moment of your death, I will be with you in the spiritual realm helping you get to the other side." The assurance that she would get help going to "the other side" comforted both Kris and Sally.

In her seminal book *On Death and Dying,* Elisabeth Kübler-Ross stressed the importance of encouraging people who are terminally ill to talk about their own death and dying. Kris, Sally and I all found value in talking about these details ahead of time. Our talks made it possible for Sally and me to know about the things that were important to Kris. We made those wishes come true. We learned her fears and gave her comfort and reassurance to the best of our abilities.

I started our conversations about the topic by saying, "Let's talk about the moment of death. I want to know what you're thinking and how you want it to be."

I asked Kris whom she wanted present at the moment she died. Did she prefer to be alone? Did she want music or not? Did it matter to her what time of day it was? Was there anything else about it that was important to her?

These were hard questions, and she never answered most of them. She consistently said her biggest concern was making sure she would get to the right place after she died. She believed that she needed help to complete the transition to "the other side." Ultimately, Kris believed everything would happen exactly as it was supposed to happen. Whenever she got scared, I reminded her of that belief.

A few days before Kris died, when she could no longer go to restaurants, she lost interest in the world. She no longer asked for food, water or cigarettes. We stopped offering her anything. For the most part, she stopped talking. She kept her eyes closed and became unresponsive to external stimuli. The earthly plane no longer held relevance for her.

She seemed to be in some other place—preparing to move to "the other side."

On April 13, Kris ate no food and stayed in bed except to use the commode. The medicines kept her pain-free, and she slept much of the day.

That evening, Sally realized there were important things she wanted to say. Even though Kris's eyes were closed and she appeared unresponsive, Sally spent time with Kris and expressed herself fully.

Sally described her last talk with Kris when Kris was too ill to respond verbally. "I talked in a tone of voice and in a way that I'd never experienced before with her or anyone. It was from the depths of my soul. It was a steady stream. I wanted to apologize for not being able to take her to the restaurants until the very end like she'd wanted. I did the best I could. I just didn't have the strength anymore. She was getting heavier and heavier, and I was getting weaker and weaker.

"I thanked her for our thousands of hours of talking and told her I would be OK. I told her we really had a ride together, and it was a great ride. I was so honored to be a part of her death and dying. It was such an incredible, unique, meaningful experience."

Sally knew Kris heard her. The next day Kris had a burst of energy. She woke up full of joy, smiling and radiant. As always, Sally kissed her good morning. Kris responded by planting kisses on every inch of Sally's face. That was the last time she had the strength to express her affection. Kris was too weak to talk, but they both felt the love between them.

When Sally told me about this talk, I recalled that scientists have found that a person's hearing is the last sense to go. That's why Hospice and medical providers encourage families to talk to their loved ones even when they appear to be comatose.

Kris stayed in bed all day and asked for nothing. She could no longer swallow her pills. The Hospice nurse came and administered a subcutaneous dose of pain medicine.

April 14 was Kris's 57th birthday. That evening, even though Kris was not conscious, Sally read aloud the birthday cards that came in the mail.

Just after midnight, the caregiver heard the shift in Kris's breathing and knew she would die soon. She went into Sally's bedroom and woke her. After putting on her robe, Sally came into the living room and sat next to the bed.

She said, "I put my arms around her the best I could and told her it was safe to go. It was amazing how peaceful, quiet and calm she was. There were no signs of distress. Then she just stopped breathing."

Sally told me later that she knew Kris's spirit had already left even though her body was still warm and she was breathing slowly. She noticed that Kris's body seemed empty. About forty-five minutes after Sally came to her side, Kris died peacefully in her sleep. Her breathing slowed and then it stopped. It was a gentle, peaceful passing.

22

IMMEDIATELY AFTER DEATH

Sally stayed with Kris for a few minutes after she died. Even though her breathing stopped, her pulse kept beating. Sally knew this was normal. She said, "It seemed like it took forever for her pulse to stop even though probably it was really a matter of moments."

Then she told the caregiver that Kris had died and asked her to stay.

Sally explained, "I didn't want to be in the house alone with Kris like that."

At 3:15 a.m., Sally called Hospice and talked with the nurse on duty. She told Sally she would call the coroner who would come soon and officially pronounce Kris dead. A coroner's job is to make sure there are no unusual or suspicious circumstances surrounding a death. Sally was instructed to gather all the unused medicines and give them to the coroner when he came. He arrived at the house around 6 a.m.

Later, I learned the coroner isn't usually involved with
Hospice patients. Funeral directors are deputized to make
official pronouncements of death. They pronounce the death
when they come to take the body. Hospice is typically the
first to be notified when death occurs, and then they contact
the funeral home director. It seems the longer the body stays
at home, the more likely the coroner will be called to
pronounce the death. Sally didn't care who made the official
pronouncement. What was important to her was to have as
few strangers as possible come to the house.

Prior to Kris's death, we talked about how long Sally
wanted to stay with Kris's body before it was removed. She
didn't know. I learned that some people keep their loved one's
body at home for more than a day to allow time for friends
and relatives to travel from out of town. Whatever people
want can be arranged. Even though Sally didn't know exactly
what she wanted, it was helpful to know she could have as
much time as she needed and wanted.

The night Kris died I was so exhausted, I never heard
my phone ring when Sally called to let me know. I checked
my voicemail when I woke up at 6 a.m. and called Sally
immediately.

I was upset that I missed the call. How could that
happen? My mind was racing, and for a moment I felt like a
failure. I took a deep breath and calmed myself. I was doing
the best I could, and that was good enough. I remembered
Kris saying it would happen exactly as it was supposed to
happen. I shifted my focus to Sally to support her.

I went to her house as quickly as I could. By the time I
arrived, the coroner had come and gone. Sally had showered

and dressed and told the caregiver she could leave. Sally and I hugged, and I listened to her tell what happened.

She offered me time alone with Kris. I sat next to her body with tears streaming down my face. I kissed her cheeks and stroked her hair. Even though she was cold and stiff, I held her hand for a short while and said the things I'd said to her so many times. I knew it was the last time I'd say those things to her.

"You're safe now. It's OK to go now. You're such a good person. You've done such good work. You've done everything you're supposed to do. Thank you for being in my life. I've learned so much from you. You'll be OK now. You'll find your way. You'll be exactly where you're supposed to be. I love you."

It was comforting to me to have that time with her. I was grateful to have time alone with her body in a totally unselfconscious way.

Two men from the funeral home came to the house with a gurney to transport Kris's body. We knew there could be no metal with her. She had stopped wearing her rings a few weeks before because her fingers were swollen. We made sure the bears and her blanket were with her.

The men said, "We're going to transfer her body to this gurney. It's not a very graceful process. You might want to go into the other room. We'll let you know when we're finished so you can come back."

They let us know when the body was transferred, and I came out to watch them roll the gurney out of the house. I felt a million tears well up inside of me as I watched them take her away.

Sally called to cancel the delivery of oxygen. A man came right away to get the oxygen tanks and pick up the hospital bed. Later that morning, two people from the funeral home came to the house to finalize the details of the service. Sally went through the motions but knew she was in no shape to make decisions. Because of our thorough planning ahead of time, there was very little she needed to do after Kris's death. There was a lot of activity all at once right after Kris died.

The coroner came to pronounce her death, funeral home personnel came to pick up her body, funeral directors came to finalize plans for the memorial service and a man came to pick up the oxygen tanks and the hospital bed. Right after Kris's death, Sally felt dazed and vulnerable. She appreciated having a supportive person with her throughout the morning.

Furman and McNabb, authors of *The Dying Time*, provide a list of things visitors can offer to do. One of those is, "When the loved one is gone, offer to help take things home from the facility or return the sickroom to a normal room in the home."

While I was at her home, I helped Sally remove the picture hooks from the living room. She said it made her feel much better to have her living room look normal again.

Later that day, I felt uneasy about where Kris's body was and what the schedule was for cremation. I called Ellen at the funeral home.

She told me, "The cremation is scheduled for three days from now. You don't need to worry. Her body is in a refrigerated room and will be treated with respect and dignity."

Hearing those words and Ellen's comforting voice helped me feel at peace.

23

BOWEL MOVEMENTS, URINE & RIGOR MORTIS

I know the title of this chapter may be startling to some readers. But I offer what I learned with the hope that it will be helpful when you are faced with caregiving during the dying time. As the dying person loses control of body functions, it helps to be prepared. End-of-life scenarios often include involuntary bodily discharge.

When Sally told me the details of Kris's death, the first thing she talked about was bowel movements. "In the last two or three weeks we were both amazed at how voluminous her bowel movements were. During that time, she'd been eating very little so it was hard to imagine there could be so much.

"The day after she stopped going out to eat, Kris stopped eating, smoking and talking. She was very weak. We wanted her to be as comfortable as possible. We put pills in her mouth and tried to get her to swallow them. She couldn't.

"The Hospice nurse was focused on preventing pain from tumors and preventing pain from constipation. She used a pain pump for the pain medicine and gave me a suppository to use with Kris on Wednesday if she didn't move her bowels by then. I gave her the suppository on Wednesday evening to prevent pain from constipation. I guess she had nothing left because nothing happened after the suppository.

"Although she slept most of the last day, she woke up to ask for help getting on the commode. Her urine was concentrated."

I arrived at their home about five hours after Kris died. When I saw Kris's body, I pulled her special blanket over her face and was surprised to notice that her lower half was wet. Later, I learned that after death, all the muscles relax and sometimes urine and stool are passed. This is more likely to happen when there is eating and drinking close to the time of death. We weren't prepared for that. Sally and I took all her wet clothes off, cleaned her up the best we could and put clean pajama bottoms on her.

We wondered if it would have been easier to change her clothes before her body got stiff. The Hospice nurse told me that even immediately after death—before rigor mortis sets in—a person's body becomes very heavy and difficult to move. I thought of the expression "dead weight."

I knew in some traditions people washed the body after death although I didn't know why. Before Kris died, when she and I talked and planned for her death, she told me she didn't want anyone touching her body unless it was necessary. At the time of our discussions, neither of us knew about the discharge that sometimes follows death.

The Hospice nurse told me, "When Hospice comes at the time of death, they offer to clean the body. Most people get great joy and pleasure while cleaning their loved one's body or brushing their hair. Other people, when asked, say, 'Nope, it's OK.' Some people don't want to get near it."

Much later, I called the funeral home and the coroner's office to learn more about rigor mortis—the stiffening of the body after death. I was told a lot of variables, including temperature and cause of death, influence the speed of body stiffening. Because of the variability, everyone I spoke with was reluctant to give me a time frame for rigor mortis.

By asking the question numerous times in various ways, I finally got the coroner to tell me, "It doesn't happen all at once, but ordinarily the body starts to get stiff in about two hours."

In general, I was told, heat speeds up rigor mortis and cold slows down the process. For example, if a person dies in the snow or a cold room, it will be slower. Most people think about a dead body getting cold. Actually, the body reaches the temperature around it. The coroner told me it had always made an impression on her to learn that if a person dies in a parking lot in Arizona during the summer, the body gets hotter after death.

As I helped Kris make this passage at the end of her life, I was struck by how much I didn't know. Some of the things I learned were predictable and others were surprising. Involuntary bowel movements, urination and rigor mortis were all part of the process.

24

THE ASHES

Many years ago my mother was in a quandary about what to do with my father's remains after his death. Before he died, my parents talked about his wish to be cremated and agreed on that plan. Neither of them thought to discuss what to do with his ashes. This oversight created an additional decision for my mother to make after his death. She wanted to follow his wishes but didn't know what he wanted.

Because they lived in Florida very close to the ocean, and the crematory could arrange to scatter the ashes into the sea from a boat, she chose that option. She came to a decision that was comfortable for her that she thought he would like, too. She said that having someone with her for moral support who approved of her decisions was a tremendous help. She knew it wouldn't have been quite as easy to do alone.

Because of my mother's experience, I wanted to be sure Kris and Sally had a plan for Kris's ashes. During our meeting with the funeral directors we asked specific questions, "Can we scatter ashes wherever we want? Is there anything we should know about scattering ashes?"

Before replying they asked if we wanted a graphic description. Kris was quick to say, "Yes." Sally and I both agreed. The funeral directors explained that cremated remains consist of light gray ash and pieces of charred bone. No metal jewelry is allowed to stay with the body during cremation. After the body is burned, the remains are ground up and placed in a stainless steel container. A plug with an identification number on it can be buried with the container or preserved as a keepsake.

The funeral directors instructed us to be sure our backs were to the wind when scattering the remains so the ashes wouldn't be blown back into our faces. If we wanted the ashes in a specific place, they told us to empty the container carefully in the designated spot. Because Kris was an avid golfer, they gave the example of scattering ashes in a sand trap on a golf course with instructions to use the rake afterwards.

While Kris was alive, we returned periodically to the topic of what to do with her ashes. We knew there were three choices.

- keep the ashes
- scatter the ashes
- some combination of the two

Neither Kris nor Sally liked the idea of keeping the ashes. Although they both wanted them scattered, they weren't sure of an appropriate final location. They wanted Kris's final resting place to be a meaningful spot that would be comforting to both of them.

Kris didn't want her ashes placed in the backyard, and she didn't want them commingled with the ashes of a beloved pet. Other than that, she wasn't sure. One day she requested that her sister, Sally and I scatter the ashes together at a favorite golf course. She liked the idea of splitting the ashes into three containers. At the time that seemed OK, and we all agreed.

After Kris died, the logistics and emotional reality of that plan no longer seemed right to any of us. For one thing, we weren't sure it was legal to scatter cremated remains on a public golf course. And even if it were legal, it would be awkward to perform that task in nice weather when other people were playing golf. We thought about waiting until a snowy, winter day; but that wasn't appealing either. The plan to scatter Kris's ashes on a public golf course wasn't viable for any of us.

Two months after Kris died when Sally was emotionally ready to part with her remains, I suggested a new idea.

Even though Kris had said she wanted her ashes scattered on the golf course, we also remembered her saying that what happens after her death was for Sally to decide.

Kris knew we had changed the menu plans for the reception after the memorial service. Originally, Sally planned to serve Kris's favorite mud pie. Later, we decided to serve healthy buffet platters of food appropriate for a luncheon.

Kris was glad Sally had made a change that would be more comfortable for her. We knew Kris would feel the same way about our change of plans for scattering her ashes.

Many months before Kris died, she arranged a cruise along the east coast for Sally and a friend. Sally participated in the planning, and it gave Kris great pleasure to give her soulmate that final gift. The date of the cruise was planned to be long after Kris's death.

Since Kris had always loved the sea and felt connected to the ocean, I suggested that Sally take the ashes with her to scatter in the Atlantic Ocean at Provincetown, Massachusetts. She liked the idea and felt relieved to have a new plan. She took a death certificate in case there were questions about the cremated remains during security checks. She never needed that document.

Prior to their departure, Sally and her traveling companion learned that there would be two other friends on the same cruise. They made arrangements for all four of them to participate in a simple ceremony. Sally brought poems to read, and they scattered Kris's remains in the ocean early one morning. Friends took pictures, and after the cruise they gave Sally a CD with a slide show on it.

When Kris was dying, I wish I had asked her more specifically which plans were important to maintain and which were OK to change.

Knowing Kris, I'm sure she would have approved of our actions. I can imagine her smiling at the thought of her remains united with the ocean she loved.

25

LIVING ON IN THE MINDS & HEARTS OF OTHERS

One Year Later

Sometimes people are surprised by the intensity of feelings that surface a year after the death of a loved one. You might experience strong feelings of anger, sadness or fear at the anniversary time. You might be somewhat numb the first year. No matter what you're feeling, it's OK and natural.

Sally's experience, considering the many memorable dates in the year following Kris's death, was similar to the experience many people have the year after a loved one dies. We talked on many occasions about her feelings and the dilemmas she faced.

Sally was overwhelmed by all the anniversaries. There were the anniversaries of Kris's death, her memorial service, her emergency surgery, her cancer diagnosis and the date she learned cancer had spread to her liver. April was the month Kris died. April was also her birthday, as well as the month Kris and Sally had celebrated their relationship anniversary for the past twenty-four years.

"Judy," she said, "Here it is Kris's birthday, and I'm treating it just like any other day."

She worried that by doing nothing she was being disrespectful. I told her, "This first year is a time to go through all the seasons without Kris and notice what's important to you."

She decided birthdays are for the living. They mark the length of time we're here. They provide a marker along the way to acknowledge our presence. They're an opportunity to think about who we are, what we've accomplished and who we are becoming.

Sally realized that her first year alone was an important time to get to know herself in a new way. She planned not to make any other major changes in her life for a while. Sally wanted to go through all the seasons without Kris and notice what was important to her.

I told Sally, "There are many anniversaries along the way, and you don't need to mark them all. There's no one right way to do this. Whatever you choose to do, or not do, is OK. It's not disrespectful or wrong to do what's right for you. Actually, it's an act of respect to pay attention to your feelings and honor them. Kris would have wanted that. You can decide to treat an anniversary like any other day, or you can treat it like a special occasion."

I continued, "Birthdays are markers and death days are also markers. They remind us how long someone has been gone. They provide an opportunity for reflection. It's OK to use that day for reflection or not."

Sally decided the date of the memorial service was significant the year it occurred but didn't have to be significant after that.

Because Sally was overwhelmed with all the anniversaries in April, I asked her, "How would it be for you, now that it's one year later, to choose one day and do something to honor and remember Kris and your relationship? This could be anything like taking a walk in the sunshine, lighting a candle, reading a poem, listening to music, inviting friends to share a meal or making a contribution to a favorite charity.

If you don't want to do anything like that this year, that's OK, too. The most important thing is to listen to yourself and be self-accepting. There's no right or wrong way to do this. The only 'should' is that you should do or not do what's right for you. Don't do things out of concern for what other people will think."

Sally decided to have a gathering of friends to honor Kris's memory and to talk about her own feelings. She scheduled it for the weekend closest to the anniversary of Kris's death. She invited each friend to bring a photo or an object related to Kris so there was a presence of Kris with them. When they were all together, Sally shared memories of her time with Kris, what she learned in the relationship and the many "gifts" she received from the process. Each person shared memories, teachings or gifts from their relationship with Kris. Then Sally read a passage she chose for the occasion.

Sally had been harboring fear that she would re-live the details of Kris's death on that anniversary day one year later.

Through our discussions, she learned she would not be disrespectful if she had a pleasant day. She was being respectful by creating a joyful day to share memories and happy times with friends.

I told Sally, "Each year when the anniversary time comes, you can expect to respond differently. That's a good thing. You're still alive. You're growing and changing. You're dreaming and doing new things, and that's the way it's supposed to be. When Kris was dying—that was *then* and this is *now*.

"A lot of people think that after a year you should be finished grieving. Don't be concerned with anyone else's timetable. There are no shoulds. If the feelings are strong for you at this anniversary time, that's OK. I'm glad you're talking with me. You can also write in your journal and revisit a grief group. I remember how valuable it was for you to attend the Hospice grief group—how much you learned there and how supported you felt. It's important to give yourself extra time and space to have your feelings.

I recommended she read Miriam Greenspan's book *Healing Through the Dark Emotions.* Anyone going through such a big loss would benefit from reading that book.

After our talk, Sally felt empowered to share her true feelings. She said, "With the help of therapy, the Hospice bereavement group and friends, I'm happier now than I've ever been in my whole life. Before Kris died, if anyone had told me that was possible, I wouldn't have believed them. I would have thought that was blasphemy! I want others to know it's possible to be happy after the death of a loved one. There are so many resources out there. Use them."

26

THE END

When I agreed to help Kris and Sally, I had no idea that this experience would affect me so profoundly. I never dreamed that I would become so deeply involved in the dying process.

While much of my time during those eleven months was spent helping them, what I learned was immeasurable. The process turned into one of the most time-consuming and exhausting experiences of my life.

I encountered moments every day when I learned something about the process of dying—and the process of living. And in turn, I learned something new about myself.

A few weeks after Kris died, I went away by myself for a week. I hadn't planned to take that time for myself, but it became clear that I needed to rest. I cried, I slept, I cried, I got a massage, I cried, I sat by the swimming pool, I cried, I swam, I walked, I wrote in my journal and I cried some more. In short, I replenished my soul.

I believe I participated in a truly profound experience and felt privileged to be part of the process. Preparing for your own death or the death of a loved one is undoubtedly difficult, but it is also one of the most meaningful and loving acts one can ever perform. Looking back, I do not regret any of it.

I've chosen to include a favorite poem of mine to conclude.

There is No Death
by Henry van Dyke

I am standing upon the seashore. A ship at my side spreads her white sails to the morning breeze and starts for the blue ocean. She is an object of beauty and strength and I stand and watch her until she hangs like a speck of white cloud just where the sea and sky come to mingle with each other.

Then someone at my side says, "There! She's gone!" Gone where? Gone from my sight, that is all. She is just as large in mast and hull and spar as she was when she left my side, and she is just as able to bear her load of living weight to her destined port.

Her diminished size is in me, not her. And just at that moment when someone at my side says, "There! She's gone," there are other eyes watching her coming, and other voices ready to take up the glad shout, "Here she comes!"

And that is dying.

▲ ▲ ▲

APPENDIX

Passing Peacefully Bill of Rights

As long as you are alive you deserve

- ▲ Relief from pain
- ▲ A place to be safe, warm and dry
- ▲ Food and drink when you want
- ▲ Help staying clean
- ▲ Help with all bodily functions
- ▲ Caring companionship
- ▲ Patience from others with your dying process
- ▲ To know that your life matters
- ▲ To be treated like you're not dead yet
- ▲ Permission from your loved ones, and yourself, to die

Please visit **www.passingpeacefully.com**
to download *Passing Peacefully Bill of Rights*.
This document is in color and suitable for framing.

REFERENCES

Mitch Albom, *Tuesdays With Morrie*. New York: Doubleday, 1997. Also available as a movie on DVD.

Sylvia Browne, *Life on the Other Side: A Psychic's Tour of the Afterlife*. New York: New American Library, a Division of Penguin Putnam Inc., 2000. www.sylvia.org.

Sylvia Browne with Lindsay Harrison, *Blessings From the Other Side*. New York: Penguin Putnam Inc., 2000. www.sylvia.org.

Ira Byock, M.D., *Dying Well: Peace and Possibilities at the End of Life*. New York: Riverhead Books, 1997. www.dyingwell.com.

Joan Didion, *The Year of Magical Thinking*. New York: Alfred A. Knopf, 2005.

Joan Furman, M.S.N., R.N., and David McNabb, *The Dying Time: Practical Wisdom for the Dying and Their Caregivers*. New York: Bell Tower, 1997.

Miriam Greenspan, *Healing Through the Dark Emotions: The Wisdom of Grief, Fear and Despair*. Boston, MA: Shambhala Publications, Inc., 2003.

Joan Halifax, *Being With Dying: Contemplative Practices and Teachings*. Audiotape Series, 1997. www.upaya.org. Available through Amazon.com

Barbara Karnes, *Gone From My Sight: The Dying Experience* (14-page booklet describing behaviors typical of one to three months before death, one to two weeks before death, days or hours before death, minutes before death). Available from Barbara Karnes, RN, PO Box 189, Depoe Bay, OR 97341.

Patricia Kelley and Maggie Callanan, *Final Gifts.* New York: Poseidon Press, 1992.

Elisabeth Kübler-Ross, M.D., *On Death and Dying.* New York: Touchstone, 1997.

Elisabeth Kübler-Ross, M.D., *The Wheel of Life: A Memoir of Living and Dying.* New York: Touchstone, 1998.

Elisabeth Kübler-Ross, M.D., and David Kessler, *Life Lessons: Two Experts on Death and Dying Teach Us About the Mysteries of Life and Living.* New York: Touchstone, 2002.

Sherwin B. Nuland, M.D., *How We Die: Reflections on Life's Final Chapter.* New York: Knopf, 1994.

Neale Donald Walsch, *Conversations With God: An Uncommon Dialogue (Book 1).* New York: G.P. Putnam's Sons, 1996.

ACKNOWLEDGMENTS

There are many people I want to thank for their love, support and encouragement during the process of making this book a reality. My editor, Joe Lewandowski, and my coach, Sam Horn, were there at the very beginning. Without either one of them, this project would never have come to fruition.

I am grateful to K-Lynn Cameron for her annual Peach Party. It was there that I reconnected with Joe shortly after Kris's death. When I told him about my profound experience working with someone who had terminal cancer, he recognized this as a valuable experience to share with everyone. He invited me to collaborate on an article. Joe is a skilled interviewer, and he wrote a compelling story that was published in the *Denver Post* and in the alternative newspaper *Weird Sisters West*. It was my work with Joe that planted the seed in my mind to write a book about this life-altering experience. Joe is a knowledgeable, thoughtful editor and a creative writer. My thanks to him for telling me I am doing "holy work."

When I attended the International Coach Federation convention, I surprised myself by wandering into an after-hours session on writing a book led by author Sam Horn. When I entered the room, I had no conscious intent to write a book. I was captivated by Sam, and by the end of the session I was entertaining two different book topics. On the flight home from the convention, I couldn't rest until I had outlined the chapters for this book. I am grateful to Sam for igniting my fire and being there for me as my coach during the two years it took me to write my story.

177

When Sam read the first draft of my early chapters, she told me this book could become an underground classic. Her undying faith in my project kept me going. She is a masterful coach, generous with her knowledge and kind in her feedback. Her guidance throughout the process was invaluable.

I am grateful to the Coaches Training Institute, where I received excellent training to keep my focus on what people want. My certification group was named "the snakes"— symbolizing transformation. For the last ten years, we have listened to and encouraged each other in our goals. Thanks especially to Steve Reiter for cheering me on as I met my writing goals for this book.

My appreciation goes to the International Coach Federation. Its yearly conferences are the most meaningful and inspiring I have attended in over thirty years of attending professional meetings.

I am lucky to have Debbie Davis in my life. As one of the first people I told about this book, she consistently encouraged me to share my story and introduced me to the e-women network of Northern Colorado writing group. My gratitude goes to Ann Clarke for leading this group and to all the women there who listened to me with rapt attention.

My thanks to Maggie Bruehlman, Patsy Barry and Dianne Wacker who shared personal experiences with me that helped me plan this book. Maggie talked about how important it was to be with her dying mother and to allow her all the time she needed to make the transition. Patsy shared the problems she experienced that resulted from equating death with defeat. Dianne gave me the idea of including suggestions for how to tell others about a terminal diagnosis.

I was fortunate to have many people express interest in reading early versions of my manuscript. Gina Chaffer, Mary Davis, Allen Drum, Jan Felker, Kay Hood, Michael Johnston,

Sydney Johnston, Ellen Jones, Carol Newlin, Sabré Page, Orly Penny and Peggy Whitt all gave me thoughtful comments on my manuscript. Each reader offered suggestions that improved the final text.

Members of my family graciously read and provided me with important feedback. My thanks to my older sister, Barbara Underwood, who contributed many hours of editing to this book. Not only did her astute comments save me from unintentionally offending others, but our work on this project healed an old wound of mine from childhood when she helped me with my homework.

I appreciate the contributions from my brother-in-law, Marty Halpern. His willingness to read my manuscript and give me a playwright's perspective on the story added a new dimension. My mother, Mildred Underwood, and her sister, Daisy Aberlin, provided a perspective that could only come from their generation.

My younger sister, Suzy Underwood, was the first to read the final version of this book. It was her eagle eye that found the last misplaced apostrophes and missing commas. Many thanks to Suzy for her chapter-by-chapter comments and her enthusiasm for this project.

My express thanks to all my relatives for telling me they're proud of me. I am lucky to come from a family with the education, talent and interest to read and critique my work in a helpful way.

I feel gratitude to Sabré Page, my yoga teacher, and the women in my Venus Yoga Circle who listened to the introduction to my book and let me know they are looking forward to reading the whole story.

My thanks to Colleen Barry for inviting me to her writing group, where the writers listened to a chapter and helped me to see where I could be more effective using dialogue instead of narrative.

I am appreciative of Allnutt Funeral Home in Fort Collins, Hospice of Larimer County and the Fort Collins Coroner's Office for answering endless questions during Kris's dying time and afterwards as I wrote this book.

Joan Welsh, friend and colleague, made the experience richer by introducing me to Sylvia Browne's work.

I am also indebted to local authors Bill West and Susan Skog for sharing their experiences of book publishing with me.

Lee Machado, graphic designer, went above and beyond the call of duty to help me when I was overwhelmed with all the tasks needing attention. I know of no one who consistently produces such gorgeous work. I appreciate Lee for being there for me in the early stages of the book design.

The folks at Lightbourne, Inc. were behind me every step of the way. Shannon Bodie provided the resolute feedback that was necessary for the creation of this striking book cover. Raina Sanderson and Bob Swingle each added their expertise. I am grateful to have had the opportunity to work with such a competent group of people.

Mary Ann Kelleher appeared in my life just when I needed her. She graciously spent many hours with me as we took turns reading the galley aloud looking for errors. Her ability to attend to every minute detail while reading aloud is impressive. I feel tremendous gratitude to her for helping me in the eleventh hour.

My heart fills with happiness when I reflect on the ongoing support and encouragement I receive from my immediate family. My life partner, Pam Gaynor, has managed to provide the perfect balance of interest and help when I needed it and distance and space when I needed that. She was the first to tell me that my writing was riveting. My daughter, Danya Underwood Rivlin, has brilliance and understanding beyond her years. She gave me valuable feedback on the entire manuscript and helped me craft a difficult paragraph so that it would be well received by her generation as well as mine. My sincerest thanks to both Pam and Danya for encouraging me to live my life in the biggest way possible.

I want to thank Sally Juday and Kris Rempfer for the profound experiences I have had with both of them. Their generous sharing of intimate details about life and death are already making a difference in the world.

Finally, I want to thank all my readers. Just as a musical conductor is nothing without an orchestra, this book is nothing without you. Thank you for reading this book and sharing it with others.

INDEX

ABOUT THE AUTHOR

Judy Underwood is a psychotherapist and life coach. Originally from New Jersey, she moved to Colorado in 1970 and earned her Ph.D. in Communication Disorders from the University of Denver. She served as a professor at the University of Northern Colorado for ten years.

In the early 1980s, she became certified as a master practitioner of Neuro-Linguistic Programming (NLP) and changed career paths. She has maintained a private practice as a psychotherapist since that time. In 1999, she became certified as a life coach from the Coaches Training Institute and holds the Professional Certified Coach (PCC) credential from the International Coach Federation. She is currently a co-leader of an international, online coaching community—Death, Dying and Legacy.

She and her life partner of more than twenty-five years live in Fort Collins, Colorado. She also enjoys spending time with her adult daughter and her family.

Dying: Finding Comfort and Guidance in a Story of a Peaceful Passing is the author's first book.

To download a free gift, please visit
www.passingpeacefully.com

To learn more about Dr. Underwood's counseling practice, please visit **www.caringcounseling.net**

To learn more about Dr. Underwood's coaching practice, please visit **www.coaching4yoursuccess.com**

FEEDBACK

Please send your stories about how this book helped you to:

Judy K. Underwood, Ph.D.
515 S. Sherwood Street
Fort Collins, CO 80521

E-mail: DrUnderwood@passingpeacefully.com
Fax: 970-482-8541

If you found this book valuable,
please encourage others to read it by posting a
five-star review of the book on Amazon.com.

Thank you.

ORDER FORM

DYING

Finding Comfort and Guidance in
a Story of a Peaceful Passing

Give this book as a gift to your friends, family and colleagues

Check your leading bookstore, visit **www.passingpeacefully.com** or order here.

Yes, I want _____ copies of *Dying: Finding Comfort and Guidance in a Story of a Peaceful Passing* for $19.95 U.S. ($24.95 CANADA) each.

SALES TAX:
Colorado residents outside Larimer County add 3% sales tax ($.60 per book). In Larimer County add 7% sales tax ($1.40 per book). Canadian orders in U.S. funds add 7% GST ($1.75 per book).

SHIPPING BY AIR:
U.S.: $4.95 for first book, $1.95 for each additional book. International: $9.95 for first book, $4.95 for each additional book.

❑ My check or money order for $_____U.S. is enclosed.
　　　Check payable to Odyssey Ink.
❑ Please charge my ❑ VISA or ❑ MasterCard.

Name _____

Shipping Address _____

City_____ State _____ Zip _____

Phone _____ E-mail _____

Card#_____

Exp. Date _____ Signature _____

Billing Address *(if different from shipping address)* _____

FAX ORDERS: 970-482-8541. Send this form.

PHONE ORDERS: 970-221-0581. Leave name, address, phone number, credit card number and expiration date.

E-MAIL ORDERS: orders@passingpeacefully.com *Do not include credit card information. Provide phone number and time zone so publisher can call to complete your order.*

POSTAL ORDERS: Odyssey Ink, Judy K. Underwood, Ph.D., 515 S. Sherwood Street, Fort Collins, CO 80521, USA

ORDER FORM

DYING
Finding Comfort and Guidance in
a Story of a Peaceful Passing

Give this book as a gift to your friends, family and colleagues

Check your leading bookstore, visit **www.passingpeacefully.com** or order here.

Yes, I want _____ copies of *Dying: Finding Comfort and Guidance in a Story of a Peaceful Passing* for $19.95 U.S. ($24.95 CANADA) each.

SALES TAX:
Colorado residents outside Larimer County add 3% sales tax ($.60 per
book). In Larimer County add 7% sales tax ($1.40 per book).
Canadian orders in U.S. funds add 7% GST ($1.75 per book).

SHIPPING BY AIR:
U.S.: $4.95 for first book, $1.95 for each additional book.
International: $9.95 for first book, $4.95 for each additional book.

❑ My check or money order for $_____U.S. is enclosed.
        Check payable to Odyssey Ink.

❑ Please charge my ❑ VISA or ❑ MasterCard.

Name _____

Shipping Address _____

City_____ State _____ Zip _____

Phone _____ E-mail _____

Card#_____

Exp. Date _____ Signature _____

Billing Address *(if different from shipping address)* _____

FAX ORDERS: 970-482-8541. Send this form.

PHONE ORDERS: 970-221-0581. Leave name, address, phone number,
    credit card number and expiration date.

E-MAIL ORDERS: orders@passingpeacefully.com *Do not include credit
    card information. Provide phone number and time zone so publisher
    can call to complete your order.*

POSTAL ORDERS: Odyssey Ink, Judy K. Underwood, Ph.D.,
    515 S. Sherwood Street, Fort Collins, CO 80521, USA

CPSIA information can be obtained at www.ICGtesting.com
Printed in the USA
266772BV00003B/1/P